# PRACTICAL  TRAINER SERIES

# *A Practical Approach to Group Training*

## DAVID LEIGH

KOGAN PAGE
Published in association with the
Institute of Training and Development

**To my Father, Nina, Tanya and the nieces**

First published in 1991

Kogan Page Limited
120 Pentonville Road
London N1 9JN

© David Leigh, 1991

**British Library Cataloguing in Publication Data**

A CIP record for this book is available from the British Library.

ISBN 07494 0414 0

Typeset by Saxon Printing Ltd, Derby
Printed and bound in Great Britain by Biddles Ltd, Guildford

# A Practical Approach
# to Group Training

**The Kogan Page Practical Trainer Series**

**Series Editor: Roger Buckley**

# Contents

## PART 2 DELIVERY AND INSTRUCTION SKILLS

# Series Editor's Foreword

Organizations get things done when people do their jobs effectively. To make this happen they need to be well trained. A number of people are likely to be involved in this training: identifying the needs of the organization and of the individual, selecting or designing appropriate training to meet those needs, delivering it and assessing how effective it was. It is not only 'professional' or full-time trainers who are involved in this process; personnel managers, line managers, supervisors and job holders are all likely to have a part to play.

This series is for all those involved with training in some way – senior personnel managers trying to link the goals of the organization with training needs, or job holders responsible for training newcomers. Therefore, the series is essentially a practical one which focuses on specific aspects of the training function. The theoretical underpinnings of the practical aspects of training are of course, not unimportant. Anyone seriously interested in training is strongly encouraged to look beyond 'what to do' and 'how to do it' and to delve into the areas of why things are done in a particular way.

The authors have been selected for their considerable practical experience. All have shared, at some time, the difficulties, frustrations and satisfactions of being involved in training and are now in a position to share with others some helpful and practical guidelines.

David Leigh concentrates on the practicalities of training groups. This involves much more than delivering training material. Many methods need to be considered in order to arrive at the most appropriate means for learning: role-playing, discussions and brainstorming, for example, all of which demand a range of skills on the part of the trainer. However, even the most skilful of trainers is not likely to succeed without thorough preparation and planning together with a concern for the 'hygiene factors' that create a good learning environment. This book is a comprehensive guide to all stages that lead to successful group training.

*Roger Buckley*

# Preface

## Is this book for you?

If you have read the title to this book in a bookshop or library and are wondering whether it will be of interest to you, the answer is probably yes. *A Practical Approach to Group Training* is:

- unashamedly practical;
- unequivocally an "approach";
- deals with training, in general; and
- concerns group training, in particular.

## What is 'group' training?

There is no mystique attached to the definition of group training. Group training is any acquisition of knowledge, skills or behaviour which involves more than two people.

This isn't to deny that the one-to-one approach doesn't serve a vital function in providing training. In fact, quite the reverse is true. The 'Sit by Nellie' method of placing an inexperienced employee alongside a more experienced one is still the most favoured method of providing on-the-job training.

(Unfortunately, the big drawback about 'sitting next to Nellie' is that the quality of training that people receive is very dependent upon the quality of your Nellie!)

## What this Book is

The purpose of *A Practical Approach to Group Training* is to provide a condensed source of practical advice and assistance, and a useful reference guide for trainers. It is hoped that it will prove particularly useful to those organizations where the responsibility for implementing training resides with managers as well as those engaged professionally in training and development.

## How to Use this Book

*A Practical Approach to Group Training* is divided into two parts:
1. Design and development
   – Concentrates on the design and development of training.
   – Includes setting objectives, developing lesson plans, selecting the appropriate training environment, and the choice of suitable training methods.
2. Delivery and instruction skills
   – Focuses on those skills which a typical trainer needs to develop in order to achieve a high standard of competency in training and development.
   – Aspects covered comprise handling questions, establishing rapport, and dealing with problem people.
   – Highlighted are the essentials of verbal and non-verbal communication, coping with stress, and evaluating the effectiveness of the training provided.

## Approach

The emphasis throughout has been placed on the practical aspects of training. To ensure that the layout of the material is consistent with this objective all the chapters follow a similar design.

---

▷             SUMMARY             ◁

Most chapters begin with a brief summary of what that chapter contains and finish with a chapter review of the key points explored.

---

## TRAINER'S TIP

In order to focus attention on helpful tips and techniques, certain areas are highlighted as a 'Trainer's Tip'. These contain advice, assistance and useful suggestions for turning facts into practical reality.

## Checklists

If you turn to the back of this book (Chapter 14) you will also find a series of checklists which provide a convenient source of reference for the many factors which need to be considered in delivering effective training. These checklists include: venue and accommodation requirements, joining instructions, materials, audio visual support, pre-course; course; and post-course.

# Part 1  Design and Development

# 1 Introduction to the Training Process

---

▷       SUMMARY       ◁

This chapter:
- Highlights the training cycle.
- Establishes the four steps to identifying learning requirements.
- Provides the foundation for setting learning objectives.

---

## The Training Process

Although training is often thought of as a *single event*, in reality planned training is a continuous process which begins with identifying the learning that is required. Figure 1.1 illustrates the training cycle process.

The initial stage, of identifying the learning requirements involved, can be further divided into four basic steps:

1. Does a problem exist? (Identifying the problem.)
2. If it does exist, is it a problem which concerns training? (Seeking a solution.)
3. Can training help? (Applying training.)
4. What should the training seek to achieve? (Setting objectives.)

## 1. Identifying the Problem

In many cases the most difficult part for any organization is recognizing that a problem exists in the first place. Once this hurdle has been overcome the problem is well on the way to being resolved.

15

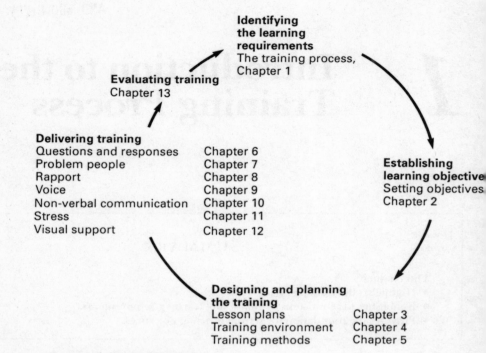

**Figure 1.1** *The training cycle*

The underlying causes of the problem may differ substantially but the ultimate effect is likely to be a reduction in quantity, a deterioration in quality and/or an increase in the costs of providing the company's goods or services.

When one of these elements exists it will be brought to the attention of the person given the responsibility of training, in one of three ways.

– Management may notice the discrepancy between the quantity or quality or costs sought and those actually obtained, and ask training for their view:

'The number of customers complaining about delayed orders has increased over the last few weeks. Do you think that this new computer system could have something to do with it?'

– Line management may believe that they have located the cause of the difficulties and ask training to rectify the situation:

'Since we installed that new computer system order processing has slowed down. Any chance of putting my people on a computer literacy course of some kind?'

– The need for training might be recognized by those responsible for providing it and an approach be made directly to the line management:

'If we introduced a training programme to familiarize your staff with the new software, you should see an increase in order processing.'

## TRAINER'S TIP

One word of caution should be voiced about relying too heavily on the line manager's impression of the organization's training needs. It is not unknown for perceptions to be unsupported by facts. A simple illustration of this can be gauged from the activities of an enthusiastic new training officer a few years ago, who introduced an audio-typing course following complaints from managers that a disproportionate amount of the manager's time was being spent in correcting typing errors in letters returned from the typing pool. It was only during the course of the training that it became apparent that the problem didn't rest with the audio typists (who demonstrated superlative audio skills) but with the managers who insisted on eating sandwiches, rustling paper and answering telephones while dictating. It was the managers with their mis-use of the equipment that warranted the training and not the long-suffering typists. The conclusion to be drawn from this tale is: always undertake a thorough investigation, or training needs analysis, before implementing any training programme.

## 2. Seeking Solutions

Merely because a problem is concerned with 'job performance' will not automatically mean that it can be rectified by training. Poor performance can be the product of a number of different factors in which training can play little or no part. For example, the deficiency can be brought about by poor design, defective materials, unsuitable working conditions or over-ambitious standards. In such circumstances management would be misguided if they were to believe that training could be a panacea for all their company's performance problems. Training for training's sake is a recipe for disaster. Training should be seen as a management tool which, when used in the correct circumstances, can significantly contribute to the company's profitability.

Common performance problems and their solutions include:

| *Problem* | *Solution* |
|---|---|
| Lack of skill | Provide suitable skill training |

| | |
|---|---|
| Insufficient knowledge | Train to broaden understanding |
| Lack of motivation | Training might re-enthuse |
| Attitudinal problems | Training can demonstrate management commitment |

## TRAINER'S TIP

The principal purpose of training is to add to the company's *effectiveness*. This should not be confused with adding to the company's *efficiency* which is something entirely separate.
**Efficiency is concerned primarily with doing *things* right, while effectiveness is about doing the *right* things well.**
It is possible for those responsible for training and development to be highly efficient in the way that training courses are run and yet still be totally ineffective by including topics irrelevant to the company or individual concerned.

## 3. Applying Training

Even in those situations where the problem identified indicates that training may provide an answer, it might still not be appropriate to undertake training.

A training 'need' can broadly be said to exist where the knowledge or skills needed by an employee to perform a task fall short of the standard of competence required. In these circumstances, while training might well be an option, there may also be a quicker, more cost effective or productive solution. For example, would it make better economic sense to recruit employees who already have the skills required rather than invest time and money in retraining existing staff? Then again, is it certain that these skills are absolutely essential for the performance of the task anyway? Could the procedure be simplified or the job 'deskilled' to a point where existing people and machinery are able to achieve the same standard of work?

One way of achieving this might be investing in advanced computer software which augments current capabilities by performing every-thing from complicated tax calculations to car diagnostics.

Assuming that training does offer the most expedient solution it is still necessary to consider the individuals involved and whether they have the capacity and commitment to benefit from the training envisaged.

## 4. Setting the Objectives

Once it has been clearly established that a problem does exist which is capable of resolution (in whole or in part) by training, then the final stage of the training process is to examine the current performance and to decide on what employees should be doing, shouldn't be doing, or should be doing differently as the result of the training. It is these performance requirements which will form the basis of any learning objectives and are of such significance that they are examined in detail in the following chapter.

---

► CHAPTER REVIEW ◄

**Training is a continuous process.**

**The training cycle includes:**

- **Identifying the learning requirements.**

- **Establishing learning objectives.**

- **Designing and planning the training.**

- **Delivering training.**

- **Evaluating training.**

**The first stage is to establish the learning requirements, in 4 steps:**

1. **Does a problem exist?**

2. **If it does exist is it a problem which concerns training?**

3. **Can training help?**

4. **What should the training seek to achieve?**

**Common performance *problems* and their training *solutions* include:**

| | |
|---|---|
| – **Lack of skill** | **Skill training** |
| – **Insufficient knowledge** | **Broaden knowledge** |
| – **Lack of motivation** | **Re-motivate** |
| – **Attitudinal problem** | **Demonstrate management commitment** |

# 2 Setting Objectives

▷                    SUMMARY                    ◁

This chapter:
- Examines the reasons for setting learning objectives.
- Explains how objectives are set and by whom.
- Establishes some guidelines for writing learning objectives.

## Why set Objectives?

The major reason for setting objectives before developing a course is that, unless you know where you are going, the chances are that you will finish up somewhere else. Consequently, setting learning objectives can:

1. Provide direction.
   Setting objectives gives a clear indication of what is to be achieved through running a particular training course.
2. Emphasize standards.
   Very often it is only when objectives are drawn up that it becomes apparent that no performance standards previously existed, or that those which did failed to reflect what could be accomplished.
3. Provide consistency.
   Line managers will be anxious to ensure that those attending

training will receive relevant instruction and that this is consistent throughout the section, department or company.

## Who Benefits from Objectives?

– Trainers.

Trainers gain a greater understanding of the desired behaviours which they are seeking to encourage and their approach can be modified accordingly.

– Trainees.

Knowing what the course entails will help to overcome any uncertainty, cynicism or hostility, and to motivate the individual.

– The Company.

Objectives indicate that training isn't an arbitrary process but one that considers the needs and requirements of the organisation. It demonstrates that training provides a quantifiable return on the time and capital invested.

## Differences between Aims and Objectives

The terms 'aims' and 'objectives' are frequently regarded as interchangeable but in practice there exists a distinct though subtle difference between the two.

When reference is made to 'aims' this invariably indicates a general purpose. It provides a direction or statement of intent. So, for example, you would 'aim' at a target but the 'objective' could be to hit the bull's eye. Whether this objective is a realistic one would depend on the people involved and the circumstances under which they operate. This means that while an 'aim' might express a desired outcome it is the objectives which will spell out how and when this is attained. You will gather from this that objectives need to be fairly explicit if they are to be effective.

## Who Decides on the Course Objectives?

Course objectives are not just conjured out of thin air, or at least they shouldn't be. For objectives to be a realistic reflection of what can be achieved and what is required, it is necessary for the objectives to be the consequence of a consultative process. In other words, the objectives set for a particular course must have been arrived at only after asking a number of interested parties. These parties include:

- Senior Management.
  Without the backing of senior management there can be little hope of acceptance of any training programme. This doesn't require the content of every course to be discussed at length with senior management but rather that the objectives of the course be agreed in outline and seen as an integral part of the company's philosophy.
- Line Management.
  As a good deal of the encouragement to participate in training is dependent on line management, it is essential that the line management should feel that there is some direct benefit from such attendance. The best way of ensuring that this commitment is forthcoming is to involve line management in developing the content and course objectives.
- Delegates.
  Last, but certainly not least, there must be support from those who will be participating in any courses. If trainees are expected to reach a specified standard within certain constraints then there must be a degree of acquiesence on their part. There is a greater chance of winning the hearts and minds of delegates once they understand what the course is seeking to achieve.

## Setting Objectives

Once this process of consultation has taken place the next step is to turn these collective aspirations into some specific learning objectives.

In order to do this the objectives proposed must satisfy certain criteria and be:

1. Realistic.
   The objectives which are set must be attainable. They mustn't be so straightforward that there is no element of challenge nor so overwhelming that their achievement seems hopeless. The best approach is to apply the laws of trajectory motion which provide that the best way of ensuring you hit your target is to aim a little beyond it.
2. Relevant.
   If the objectives are going to have any meaning they must be

seen to have direct relevance to the individual. This can either mean that they will have an impact on work performance now or in the future, or that they will have some influence on the trainee's personal development.

3. Positive.

   It follows that if objectives are to have direct relevance they must also be of benefit to the individual. Consequently, objectives are drafted to provide a positive outcome rather than stipulating what a trainee will no longer do as the consequence of attending a course.

4. Certain.

   Vague objectives are no objectives. Objectives should clearly specify who will achieve what, by when and under what circumstances. They should also state how success will be measured and any cost or time constraints involved.

5. Justifiable.

   No matter how laudable the objectives of a course are, the true measure of their success is seen by many companies in financial terms. Unless it can be demonstrated that the organization will receive some return on its investment in training the course will be regarded as an unnecessary drain on company funds.

## Writing Learning Objectives

For any learning objective to be effective it must comprise three elements:

1. An observable action.
2. A measure of performance.
3. The relevant conditions.

1. An observable action

   Any objective should set out behaviourial requirements which can be independently observed. This is necessary because unless the activity can be objectively assessed the effectiveness of the training cannot be gauged.

   The best method of selecting this activity is by identifying what it is that you would want the course participants to be able to do once the course has been completed: 'On completing the course delegates will be able to . . .' The missing verb will provide the learning outcome. For example: bake a cake; write a report; mend a fuse.

23

2. A measure of performance
Incorporated in the objective must be some indication of the standard of performance required. So that any course participant can be sure about how the task must be performed:
   - What frequency must be achieved?
   - What quality must be attained?
   - What accuracy will be expected?

3. Relevant conditions
The objectives should set out the parameters or circumstances under which the standards should be fulfilled. So that, for example, when setting the requirements for typing a letter the objectives might read:

On completion of the course trainees will be able to:
   - type a given letter (observable action).
   - with no more than five typing errors (measurement of performance).
   - within 20 minutes and using a 'Gizmo 500' computer (relevant conditions).

Other relevant conditions might be:
   - Assemble equipment 'using a standard 6mm screwdriver'
   - Service machinery 'without recourse to the manual'
   - Wire a plug 'in accordance with the safety code'
   - Solve a problem 'using techniques demonstrated'.

## Clarifying Objectives

The purpose of setting objectives is to establish what is to be accomplished by attending the course and providing a discernible standard for trainees to gauge performance. This means that measurement and conditions must be unequivocal.

Suitable action words include:

| | |
|---|---|
| Calculate | Identify |
| Categorise | Indicate |
| Clarify | Name |
| Define | Rank |
| Distinguish | Specify |
| Find | State |
| Highlight | Stipulate |

Words which should be avoided when drafting learning objectives are:

Acquaint                    Know
Appreciate                  Realize
Comprehend                  Understand
Familiarize

All these words are incapable of external assessment. If you ask someone if they '*understand* how visual support can assist the trainer,' they may say they do because:

- they don't want to hurt your feelings;
- they genuinely believe they do when they don't;
- they don't like to admit that they haven't understood.

If the measurement is '*describe* three ways visual support can assist the trainer', then if they (a) cannot describe anything, (b) only describe two ways, or (c) the items described aren't visual – then they haven't achieved the objective.

Why they haven't been able to satisfy the objective might be something that will need to be established, but what is clear is that the performance standard hasn't been reached. Measurable criteria include:

- 'within two decimal places . . .'
- 'not more than 20 minutes . . .'
- 'no greater than . . .'
- 'without deviating more than . . .'
- '90 per cent success . . .'
  'only 1 in 10 . . .'

| Trainee | Verb or action | Object | Measurable criteria | Conditions |
|---------|----------------|--------|---------------------|------------|
| Junior Typist | Copy Type | Letter | Without more than 5 mistakes | in 20 minutes using word processor and dictionary |
| Book-keeper | Prepare | Bank reconciliation | Achieving an accurate balance | Using: calculator and documentation |
| Telephonist | Hold, connect or transfer | All telephone calls | without cutting off, or misconnecting more than 1 call in 5 | on a 'Widget 50' PABX and using a telephone directory and organizational chart |

**Table 2.1** *Examples of objectives*

► CHAPTER REVIEW ◄

**Reasons for setting objectives:**

- – Provides direction.

- – Emphasizes standards.

- – Provides consistency.

**Guidelines for setting objectives are that they should be:**

| | | |
|---|---|---|
| Realistic | Positive | Justifiable |
| Relevant | Certain | |

**When writing learning objectives they should contain three elements:**

1. An observable action.

2. A measure of performance.

3. The relevant conditions.

**Examples of actions include:**

| | |
|---|---|
| Calculate | Highlight |
| Categorize | Identify |
| Clarify | Name |
| Define | Rank |
| Distinguish | Specify |
| Find | State |
| | Stipulate |

# 3 Developing a Lesson Plan

▷            SUMMARY            ◁

- The importance of developing a lesson plan.
- What this plan should include.

If the group is going to obtain the maximum benefit from the training it receives it is imperative that the training experience is designed to make learning as easy as possible. This means that you should have a very clear idea of what you are seeking to achieve by running the training and how you intend to reach these goals.

It might well be that you decide to adopt the traditional, structured approach – setting out the learning points in order, together with the proposed method of attaining them. Alternatively, it may seem more appropriate to opt for a less rigid format, where the opportunity to decide on the means of direction of learning is delegated to the group.

These are, of course, two opposite ends of the scale and there is nothing preventing any course incorporating aspects of either approach in the final course design.

## Why is a Lesson Plan Necessary?

Whether your preference is for a controlled or flexible approach to training, there will still be a need to set certain parameters in advance. Even the most informal training programme will need to define learning objectives and consider the time and resources available.

There are a number of reasons for preparing a lesson plan. First, it focuses the trainer's and group's attention on the areas which require the greatest emphasis. Second, it ensures that adequate account is taken of the resources available and that these are utilized to the full. This is particularly true of one of the most scarce training resources – time. Setting out a lesson plan and including rough timings will help to keep the group on track and prevent the programme becoming over-ambitious. Third, it provides a means of verifying that nothing has been overlooked, underemphasized or misjudged.

Merely the *existence* of a lesson plan can have positive effects. Many course participants find training a daunting prospect, and setting out guidelines will go some way to putting them at ease. It will provide them with clear goals and set out what expectations the trainer has for them. As long as these expectations are realistic this will help to motivate the individuals in the group.

## What Should be Included?

In Chapter 1 we looked at setting objectives for training, and now that we have established the role of a lesson plan, the next step is to consider the route to achieving these objectives.

Later chapters will look at the methodology of disseminating knowledge (the how we do it) but at this stage we are simply examining the knowledge itself (what knowledge are we trying to communicate?).

In essence the knowledge can be seen as different layers of an onion, or rings on a target, broken down into three principal classifications: information that the group *must* know, information that the group *should* know and information that the group *could* know. (See Figure 3.1.)

### The Three Classifications of Information

#### Must know
These are items of information which are essential to the understanding of the topic in question. In most cases they will have already been identified in any training needs analysis and as they are fundamental to the success of any training course on the subject they must be given the highest priority. Areas which could fall within the 'must know' category might include, safety rules, legislative requirements, hygiene requirements.

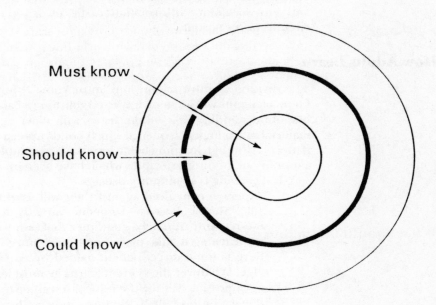

**Figure 3.1** *Three classifications of information*

### *Should know*

Information which trainees 'should know' would include anything which relates directly to the information in the 'must know' category and elaborates or expands upon it. For example, this might include other practices and procedures which interlink with those required for safety reasons or hygiene practices which are important but non-statutory.

### *Could know*

The 'could know' matters are those which can be described as useful to the group but largely incidental to the subject. These are items of information which, if time permits, could provide a useful background to the topic but will not directly assist in its effective execution. Illustrations of this category would include historical details, broader aspects of the task, further areas of interest, and general information.

The classification of information into these three categories allows each aspect of the subject to be examined and assigned to the appropriate category. In this way it is possible to provide a degree of prioritization, enabling all the essential elements to be covered in the time available, and any secondary information to be incorporated as and when circumstances permit.

## How Adults Learn

The division of information into 'must know', 'should know', 'could know' elements will go some way to establishing a balanced lesson plan, but understanding *how* adults learn will allow us to structure the material into a logical sequence which builds upon a person's learning pattern. Although learning behaviour is a very complex issue, there are a number of guiding principles which have been established:

1. Learning is a voluntary process.

   'A person convinced against their will, is of the same opinion still.' Merely because someone attends a training course doesn't, unfortunately, guarantee that they will learn anything. For learning to take place, the trainee must be convinced that there is some direct benefit gained by acquiring that knowledge. Whatever the student learns he must learn personally. It is not possible yet for the reluctant trainee to engage someone to learn on his behalf. No one can learn for him if he doesn't want to. This means that while it is the student's attitude which will decide how much is learnt, it is the trainer's job to make him want to. The onus is on the trainer to make the subject matter interesting and relevant so that everyone attending receives something of benefit.

2. Responsibility increases learning.

   The good news is that recognizing that the individual controls whether they learn and at what speed, will in itself increase the learning process. Where the trainer has passed over the responsibility for learning to the individual concerned there has been a measurable increase in both the amount learnt and the extent of knowledge retained.

3. Learning builds on existing knowledge.

   Adults learn by taking current knowledge and using it as a foundation to build on. The adult capacity to learn is to a great extent dictated by the range of experiences the individual possesses. This is why it is so important to gain some insight into the background and qualification of those attending the courses for the training to succeed.

4. Learning moves from the simple to the complicated.
   If adult learning is dependent on existing knowledge it makes sense to start from the basics and work up gradually to more complicated concepts. If a trainer launches into difficult areas too early he risks losing or alienating the student completely. The lesson plan should guide the trainee through the material step-by-step, grafting new knowledge on to old and verifying that this has been fully understood before moving forward.
5. Each person learns at his or her own pace.
   Although the trainer provides the learning environment it is the individual who dictates the rate of learning. The trainer can influence the pace by putting trainees of approximately equal ability together or by changing the balance of skills completely, but whether this has any effect will ultimately depend on the people involved.
6. Adults learn best by doing.
   Adult learning increases in direct proportion to the amount of participation that takes place. This means that any lesson plan must provide opportunities for the group to test their understanding at regular intervals. This involvement may be achieved by role playing, case studies, games or simulations (see Training Methods).

## Other Learning Plan Considerations

So far we have examined two major areas which will influence any lesson plan. These are:

1. Those areas which trainees need to know and the degree of importance attached to this material.
2. The way in which adults learn and the best way of reflecting this in the course structure.

There are, of course, a number of other factors which will have an impact upon the structure and content of any training course. These include:

1. Level of understanding.
2. Course size.
3. Availability of equipment and materials.
4. Financial constraints.
5. Timing.

### Level of understanding

As adult learning is built on to a trainee's existing knowledge (sometimes referred to as his or her 'Cognitive Inventory'), adequate account must be taken of the depth of knowledge and length of experience already attained by those attending.

### Course size

The number of people taking part will affect how much can be accomplished and what facilities and trainers are necessary. As a general guide the larger the size of the group the slower the pace of learning. The lesson plan should indicate the optimum number of trainees who should participate and where there is a minimum or maximum number necessary this should be also clearly stated.

### Availability of equipment and materials

Another factor which must be considered in putting a lesson plan together is what materials are available and how accessible the equipment is. To some extent this will be tied in with the financial costs of providing such items but, irrespective of this, the lesson plan should give a realistic indication of the material and equipment needed to undertake the course.

As with all facilities the approach should be to set out the ideal course requirements and to recognize that there might be limitations on their provision.

### Financial constraints

One of the most potent influences on the training provided will be the cost involved. In producing the lesson plan the designer should aim to satisfy the course objectives at the lowest cost feasible. This doesn't mean that the course should cut corners or be governed by cost factors alone. The aim of the course is to satisfy the training objectives and achieve the highest standard of training possible at a cost that is acceptable to the organization. If the objectives of the course cannot be achieved within the limits of the available budget then it is better not to run the course at all than to run it unsuccessfully.

### Timing

There is rarely enough time to cover everything you would want to, and to the depth you would like, on any training course. The essential thing is to use the time available to good effect and not to over-estimate what can be accomplished during this period. The trainer's natural tendency towards optimism can have drastic consequences when dealing with time schedules.

There will always be a period of non-productive time on any training course. Account must be taken of this during the course design, in order to ensure that major learning points do not occur at points where the group will be at their least attentive.

## TRAINER'S TIP

A rough guide to non-productive time should include:
- Orientation time – 20 minutes
  This should be allowed at the beginning of each course to give group members the opportunity to acclimatize to their new surroundings and to take account of any late arrivals. Use this time to help the assimilation process by setting out the course programme, explaining any housekeeping requirements and introducing the trainer, the course objectives and each group member. A short ice-breaking exercise might also be introduced where this seems appropriate.
- Settling down time – 5 minutes
  Allow five minutes following each break for the group to settle back into learning mode after socializing. This time can be used for summarizing the points covered so far, or to introduce the sessions about to begin.
- Breaktimes – 15-20 minutes
  Ensure adequate provision is made for coffee/lunch/tea breaks and that this estimate is fair considering any distance or queuing involved. If the group feel that your estimate is unrealistic they will ignore it *and all subsequent timings*. As a rule of thumb most refreshment breaks are 15-20 minutes plus resettlement time. Lunch will depend on the menu and the venue.
- Stretch breaks – 5 minutes plus re-settlement
  Where the material covered is complicated or intense, consider providing stretch breaks to counteract the descending learning curve as well as giving the group members an opportunity to relax or to address their natural needs. If stretch breaks are to be included, inform the group in advance and this will prevent their attention being diverted elsewhere.
- Miscellaneous – 20-30 minutes
  Take into account any time lost throughout the day on answering questions, dealing with problems, setting up equipment or handing out material. If there is any time remaining at the end of the day don't waste it, use it for recommending further reading, covering questions or providing a review.

To maintain close control over the time, check that a large, accurate clock is on the back wall opposite you during training (or alternatively a free-standing desk clock can serve the same role). The clock should be obvious to the trainer but not so apparent to the group. On no account should the trainer keep control by looking at his or her wristwatch, as this is likely to produce corresponding behaviour in members of the group.

To make the available learning time more productive the lesson plan should also take into account those periods where concentration is at its peak and aim to make these coincide with the more demanding parts of the course. (See Figure 3.2.)

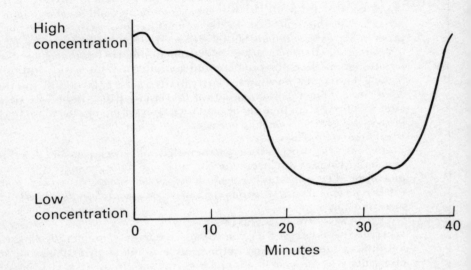

**Figure 3.2** *Group's concentration graph*

This would provide the following learning structure to the day:

– Opening session – Morning break
   Earlier on, lightweight, scene setting. Later laying down the foundation for future sessions and covering areas already aware of.
– Morning break – lunchtime
   Period best suited to heavyweight material. Introduce concepts, build on pre-existing knowledge, challenge thinking.
– Post lunch – afternoon break
   Overcome post-lunch inertia by a short, dynamic session. Participative exercises, discussions, high impact session. Followed by brief refresher of morning session to reinforce learning before expanding on areas covered. Keep the session punchy both in content and style.

– Afternoon break – close
> Lighter activities, but don't wind down too early. Include reviews, action plans and commitments to change before drawing to a close.

## Putting Together a Lesson Plan

Lesson plans appear in a variety of forms and guises with titles ranging from 'Training Schedule' to 'Instruction Guide' but all of them serve the same purpose and contain the same basic components.

They exist to clarify firstly *what* is to be taught and then to set out *how* this will be communicated. In each case the lesson plan can be divided into three elements made memorable by all beginning with C. These are:

– Commencement.
– Core.
– Conclusion.

An example of a lesson plan outline is shown in Table 3.1 (see page 39).

### Commencement

The first task of the commencement is to establish a suitable title for the course or session.

– Title: The title must be specific and describe the skill being taught or the information being conveyed. Avoid broad titles which might lead others to believe areas of the topic will be included when they cannot be in reality.

> It should also be apparent from the title exactly who will benefit from attending the course.

> Titles such as 'Finance' give little information. Instead the title could be 'Finance for the Non-Financial Manager', which clearly establishes the subject, the content and the level of knowledge necessary to attend.

– Objectives: Setting out the objectives will provide further guidance on what will be included in the course or session. These objectives will be based on those identified at the analysis stage and should be reviewed to ensure that they take adequate account of the target audience.

> It is a common error for trainers to have unrealistic aspirations and to over-estimate the amount of material which can be covered successfully in any course or session.

– Introduction: The next step is to consider what matters ought to be incorporated into any introduction. These could be:

1. Set the scene
   This should state what the course is about, and what will and what won't be covered on the course.
2. Show relevance
   Explain the reasons why the course is being run and the benefits that are envisaged by attending. It is important to emphasize that these benefits shouldn't be restricted to reasons why the *company* feels the subject is important but rather it should clearly highlight the direct or indirect benefits which present and future participants will receive. These might include increased opportunity, greater job satisfaction, improved conditions, or more job security.
3. Arouse interest
   People learn best when they are interested. Put this to good effect by demonstrating as early as possible that the course will be interesting, enjoyable and instructive. Make people feel that they are fortunate to have the opportunity to attend the training and that they dare not miss a single syllable.
4. Relax the group
   Many people find attending training a nerve-racking experience. If they have been forced into attending they might be concerned about what they have been coerced into. If they attended voluntarily they will need confirmation that they have made the right decision. In either case it is for the trainer to win them over and to gain the group's support.

   In most cases this isn't difficult to achieve because, in the majority of cases, the group *want* to believe that they are going to get some advantage and enjoyment from attending. Merely giving voice to the group's fears and showing you understand what they might be going through is, in many cases, enough to win the group over.
5. Give your background
   Briefly give some information about yourself as course trainer and, where possible, explain what specific qualities make you suitable to run the course. Be careful not to oversell your abilities. Doing so can make you sound conceited or may be viewed as a belief that you need to justify your position.
6. Give course programme
   An outline of the programme will assist in relaxing the group.

Run through each of the main sections and summarize the key points in just a couple of sentences. If you wish to provide a written programme, avoid making any reference to timings as these can be unduly restrictive and cause difficulties later on.

7. Hygiene factors

    The introduction is also the time to explain any rules on smoking, check for special dietary requirements, complete any documentation and sort out room allocations.

8. Participants' introduction

    Finally, give the group an opportunity to introduce themselves. This can be by the traditional 'name, job, background' approach, or by setting up some form of 'ice-breaking' exercise.

## Core

The core of the lesson plan comprises and sets out the detailed subject matter of the course and, in order to do this justice, a good deal of thought should be given to what to include and how to present it. This is the most crucial part of the lesson plan.

What goes into this part of the plan will be dictated by the course that you are running and will vary accordingly. Nevertheless there are some guidelines for developing the lesson plan core.

1. Research the subject.

    Research your subject thoroughly. Make sure that you have collected all the material, data, latest information necessary to present the course with confidence.

2. Establish the main elements.

    Distil from this material the central strands which run through the subject area.

3. Categorize these elements into those topics which the trainees:

    – must know
    – should know
    – could know

    according to the criteria laid down earlier in this chapter. Those areas classified as 'must know' become session objectives which have to be achieved in order to reach the minimum standards necessary for competency in the subject. Topics regarded as 'should know' ought to receive a passing mention even where time constraints prevent discussion in detail.

4. Allocate time.

    With these objectives in mind, begin to consider how much time needs to be attributed to each of these elements in order to cover them to the depth required.

5. Organize material

The most time-consuming stage is organizing the material into a logical sequence within the time available. This should follow the learning rules set down earlier with new information building on old and moving from simple ideas to more complicated concepts.

It is also during this stage that the material should be grouped together into blocks and thought should be given to the most suitable teaching method to develop this material (see Chapter 5). These blocks should follow on from each other and introduce a new topic each time.

---

## TRAINER'S TIP

One simple method of accomplishing this is to write each topic that the course participants 'must, should or could' know, on to separate plain 6″ × 4″ (150 × 100mm) record cards or quarto sheets of paper.

It is then possible to experiment with the order of each of the learning points by moving the cards around until a logical thread or pattern is established. When this has been achieved, the final order can be included in your lesson plan.

---

6. Review.

Once stages 1 to 5 have been completed, time should be taken to consider the core structure and to check that there is a natural sequence between each of the blocks and that they meet their learning objectives.

## Conclusion

The final part of the lesson plan is the conclusion. This should draw together any loose threads from the course by providing a review of the points covered. It is an opportunity to answer questions, clarify doubts, recommend further reading and point the way to the future. It is important that the course should leave the group feeling motivated and confident. There should be a feeling of completeness about the course so that no one feels that there are things left unanswered or areas uncovered.

## TRAINER'S TIP

There is no rule that says that a lesson plan must be *written* in a logical sequence, only that it must *follow* a logical sequence. This means that if it is difficult to think about the introduction to a course, leave it to the end and use the ending as inspiration for the commencement. If you do this you will find that not only is this easier, it can also be a very effective way of lending symmetry to the whole course.

Programme: Management Skills          Course Date: 17-20 March 2001
Course: Effective Problem Solving      Venue: Training Centre
   for Management
Level: Novice (Recent Promotions)      Trainer: Charlotte Moss
Session: Brainstorming. Day 1 11 am - 12 noon

Objectives: On completing this session participants will be able to:
1. Identify the situations where brainstorming can be used.

2. Explain the process and procedure for brainstorming (including the 6 'rules' of brainstorming).

3. Demonstrate these principles in practice by conducting a 20-minute brainstorming exercise on a given topic without contravening any of the rules.

| Action | Issue | Equipment |
| --- | --- | --- |
| 11.00 *Ask* Group | This session looks at 'Brainstorming' | Flipchart headed 'Brainstorming' |
| *Write* up answers | – | Pens and flipchart |
| *Show* group | 'Brainstorming is a method of generating ideas' | Slide 1 'Man with lightbulb above head' |
| Explain | The process works best if you follow 6 ground rules | |
| *Show* group | '6 ground rules of brainstorming' | Slide 2 No criticism Equal participation Free association Encourage ideas Record all ideas Incubate results |
| *Distribute* | Exercise 1 | Handout |

**Table 3.1** *Example lesson plan*

► CHAPTER REVIEW ◄

**A Lesson Plan:**

- Emphasizes key areas.
- Identifies available resources.
- Prevents areas being overlooked.
- Establishes what is required by trainer and trainee.

**Three elements of a Lesson Plan. Information that the group:**

- Must know.
- Should know.
- Could know.

**Adults learn best when:**

- The training is voluntary.
- Individuals carry the responsibility to learn.
- The knowledge is built on past knowledge.
- The learning moves from the simple to the complex.
- Individuals learn at their own pace.
- Opportunities exist to learn by doing.

**Factors affecting the structure:**

- Level of understanding.
- Course size.
- Available equipment and materials.
- Financial constraints.
- Timing.

**A Lesson Plan comprises:**

Commencement.

Core.

Conclusion.

# 4 The Training Environment

▷ **SUMMARY** ◁

This chapter:
- Identifies in alphabetical order some of the key factors which influence the choice of training venue and contribute to the excellence of the training provided.

To a large extent the most suitable environment for training depends on the type of training that is being undertaken (see Chapter 5). Even though it has been said that all we need is 'a log, someone with a question and someone to help find the answer', there is a great deal more that can be done to provide the best training environment. Set out below are just some of the factors which must be considered when selecting a suitable training venue. This list has been compiled in alphabetical order for convenient future reference. It is not intended to be exhaustive but it should provide a useful starting point for those organizing training courses (see also Chapter 14: Checklist).

## Accommodation

Where the course is intended to be residential, considerable thought must be given to the accommodation for the trainees as well as for the training itself. Accommodation must be comfortable, functional and as spacious as possible.

If the course is going to require some work to be undertaken by trainees independently in the evenings, then it is important that each room has a desk, table lamp and is free from distracting noise or bustle.

Most conference centres, hotels or purpose-built training centres seem to provide a good standard of accommodation and it is essential, if trainees are to participate fully on the course, that they also have ample opportunities to relax or wind-down. Ideally a venue with sports or leisure facilities would be advantageous but at the very minimum residential courses should provide individual televisions or TV lounge, tea/coffee-making facilities and access to the telephone.

## Bar

As a general rule the maxim 'when the wine is in, the wit is out' is very appropriate for training courses. Drink and training don't mix. This doesn't mean that there shouldn't be an opportunity for groups, particularly on residential courses, to let their hair down and relax but rather that there should be a clear line of demarcation separating these opportunities from the training input. Where the course is residential, a bar is often the ideal location to review the events of the day and to provide a forum for socializing and discussion.

Drinking in the lunch breaks, however, should be discouraged wherever possible. (The post-prandial training session is a difficult one at the best of times and if half the group is comatose this is made even harder.)

## Car Parking

If the course venue is remote, or a large number of people are likely to travel by car, sufficient car parking facilities should be made available. It might not be possible to *reserve* spaces for the course members but there must be adequate spaces for all those attending. If special arrangements need to be made these must be set out in joining instructions together with a map indicating the location of the car parks (and any requirements which need to be fulfilled – pay and display, advance reservations, etc).

## Ceilings

Ceiling heights, like the size of the room itself, can often have a significant effect on the success of the training provided.

If the ceilings are too low the room can feel oppressive. On the other hand, if they are too high the room can seem cavernous and sound echoes around in the rafters, making it difficult to hear.

The optimum height appears to be 10ft (3m) – sufficiently high to ensure that when the temperature rises so does the heat but not so large that the sound escapes with it.

## Chairs

The common chair can have an impact on training which far exceeds its importance as a piece of furniture.

Research seems to provide ample support to show that the seat of learning is directly affected by the physical seating. Or to put it another way, there appears to be a correlation between the absorption of the brain and the comfort of the bottom.

This means that it is imperative that care is taken, where possible, to provide comfortable seating. The seating selected should have a slightly dished area for the bottom and sufficient width to be accommodating. Avoid plastic or vinyl chairs, which cause the body to sweat. Nylon seat covers might be easily maintained but that doesn't make them any more suitable for sitting on. The favoured seating is padded fabric or materials that do not conduct cold or heat.

The design of the chair can also be significant. Chairs with seats that slope back or have a protruding metal frame can cut off the circulation to the legs if used for long periods. Ideally, seating should be 17" (430 mms) from the floor and with a minimum of an inch of padding on the seat and back. When working out the room layout remember to take

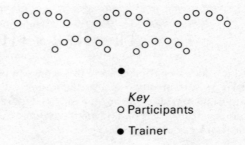

Key
○ Participants

● Trainer

**Figure 4.1** *Arc of chairs*

account of the number of chairs required and the space that will be needed for access to them (see Figure 4.1).

Where rows of seating are called for there will be a great deal more interaction if the rows are broken down into groups of six to eight rather than one long row of twenty-four. Further involvement can be achieved by using individual chairs rather than chairs which are fixed to the floor or to each other and by setting these out in arcs rather than lines.

Finally, always provide enough chairs for all course participants plus a few spare chairs for latecomers, observers and unexpected visitors.

## TRAINER'S TIP

Obviously the type of seating available is not always something within the trainer's control but the programme is. If you have any doubt about the effect that sitting for long periods will have on a group, design a programme which includes ample opportunity to move around or take stretch breaks.

This is particularly important where the course participants would not usually be required to sit down for long periods in order to carry out their jobs – for example shop assistants, meter readers, etc.

## Disabled

Where training courses are likely to be attended by trainees with disabilities or special needs these must be taken into account. One of the prime concerns will be accessibility. Will it be necessary to have

## TRAINER'S TIP

Many difficulties, such as partial hearing or vision, can be overcome with a little forward planning. Placing group members nearer the trainer will often compensate substantially.

It is also important to realize that anyone can need special care. One training department in a media company calculated that during the skiing season at least two members on any course had broken legs or back problems!

ramps or special equipment? Is there a lift? Other factors often overlooked include toilet facilities, parking spaces and meal-time arrangements.

Groups requiring special care include those who are deaf or blind, those with impaired hearing or vision, and those with other special needs.

## Electrics

Do verify that the training venue has sufficient electrical points for all your needs – not only that they exist, but that they are in a form and location that you want. If you will be using a video player and a television monitor you are likely to require at least a double socket point.

You may also feel that where computer facilities are being used that a socket wired directly to the mains would be advisable rather than risking power surges by other electrical appliances cutting in and out and putting your data in jeopardy.

Certain venues require that all electrical installations be undertaken or checked by their own electrician. These might include lights, projectors or sound equipment and, if so, provision should be made for this beforehand. Do check that any electrical appliances are adequately fused, that spare fuses are available and that the electrical installation is able to support equipment of the nature and type being used.

## TRAINER'S TIP

An extension reel or lead is a valuable addition to any trainer's equipment list. There can be few things quite as infuriating as an unbridgeable gap between the plug on a piece of electrical apparatus and a socket set in the wall.

## Equipment

Most training courses make use of equipment of some kind and a detailed list of equipment needed to run the course successfully ought to be drawn up in advance and where necessary sent to the venue.

The most common equipment needs include:

Flip charts

Writing paper

Spare flip chart pads

Pencils

Pens (permanent and
whiteboard)

Tent cards

Badges

See 'Checklist' section for more information.
The more specialist equipment might include:

TV Monitor

Projectors

Video playback
facilities

Carousels

Overhead projector

Video camera

Screens

Audio equipment

Computers

Particular course equipment:

Team development games

Safety equipment

Telephone simulation packs

The best approach is to establish exactly what equipment you will need
and notify the appropriate parties accordingly. Stipulating the equipment you need will not eliminate all the problems but it will prevent a
U-Matic video player being supplied to play a VHS video tape, and vice
versa.

## TRAINER'S TIP

The general rule that you should never make assumptions is a good maxim to follow when
considering equipment.

Never assume that equipment such as photocopiers or word-processors will be available
or accessible.

Never assume that computer systems will be compatible. Check first.

## Fire and Fire Drills

Most hotels, conference facilities and training rooms test their alarms
or safety drills on a regular basis. Enquiries should be made to find out
in advance what and when these are.

Innumerable training courses have been interrupted at a crucial
point by the high-pitched wail of a fire alarm.

If a test is expected, the trainer should notify the group of the fact beforehand and avoid any unnecessary anxiety.

Whenever an alarm is sounded the safest response is always to evacuate the building. The trainer should act decisively and direct the group calmly and quickly to the nearest exit. Lifts should be avoided and belongings left behind.

Steps should also be taken to notify the group of the drill early on and to reinforce the importance of keeping entrances and exits clear.

Particular consideration should be given when disabled members of the course are present.

## TRAINER'S TIP

It is worth mentioning that as well as the more obvious reasons for caring about safety, there is also an incidental message to course members, which is that the safety of the group is something the trainer values, and this can help develop greater empathy with the group.

## First Aid

An adequate First Aid pack should be available irrespective of the type of training being undertaken. Where the training involves particular hazards it may be necessary to provide additional equipment or to formulate a plan to deal with possible problems.

The First Aid kit should be readily accessible and not locked away. Its location should be well known or identified. Always check it regularly and replace any items out of date or used.

Headaches or migraines are a frequent occurrence on training courses and an effective trainer should maintain control over an adequate supply of suitable proprietorial remedies. Other items which should be provided include: bandages, Elastoplasts, antiseptic, scissors, eye bath, cotton wool and tweezers.

## Food

The influence that food can play in the success or otherwise of a training course far exceeds the actual time spent consuming it. It is an upsetting truth that participants will remember with greater clarity the food they ate on a course than the name of the trainer who ran the course. It can be a humbling experience to realize that the most vivid memory many participants will have of your course will be the sherry trifle.

This knowledge does mean, however, that time invested in getting the food correct is time well spent. Take care to ensure that the quality and cooking of food is to a high standard. Wherever possible ensure that there is a choice of dishes and in particular that there are alternative vegetarian dishes for non-meat eaters.

Include a question in any joining instructions about any dietary requirements so that advance notice can be provided to catering staff. Special diets aren't the exclusive province of vegetarians. There may be medical requirements such as high fibre, low sodium meals. Equally there may be religious preferences.

Wherever a special diet is requested take care to handle this diplomatically. Many people are self-conscious about what they eat and questions at the beginning of the course can be a little intimidating as well as embarrassing.

Where there is some control over the meals selected try to limit heavy meals which may make the group lethargic afterwards.

## Layout

Getting the room layout right can contribute significantly to the enjoyment and participation on the course. As mentioned previously (see Chairs) placing group members in rows will reduce the interaction between people, while setting chairs in an arc will increase discussion, eye contact and overall enjoyment.

### TRAINER'S TIP

It is also a useful practice to draw up a room layout diagram for each of the different courses that are run. This can be sent, where appropriate, to the training venue at the same time as any confirmation and can remain on file until the room is set up for the course.

Some of the more common seating layouts are shown in Figures 4.2 - 4.12.

The most suitable table and seating layout will depend on the nature of the training provided, the number of people attending and the

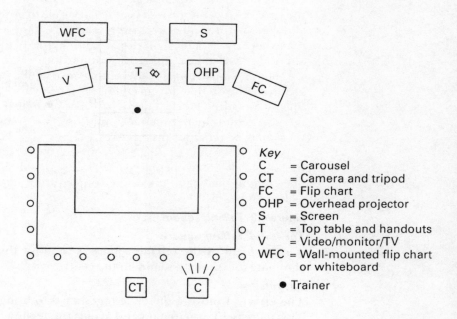

**Figure 4.2** *A typical training room layout*

facilities available to you. Figure 4.3 shows the square arrangement, which is popular where a degree of formality is necessary.

### The Square Arrangement
#### Advantages
Allows a large number of participants to discuss issues. The difficulty in identifying where the *top* of the table is means that all positions can be regarded as equal.

#### Disadvantages
Difficult to make eye contact with all participants.
Not suitable for less formal occasions.

#### Suitable for
Discussions, single team development.

49

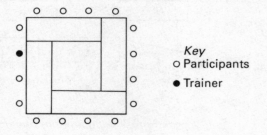

**Figure 4.3** *Talking square*

### The 'solid' talking square

A refinement of the talking square is to move the table together to eliminate the 'no-man's land' in the centre.

*Advantages*

The effect of moving the table together is to bring both sides closer. This increases participation and avoids the feeling that the parties are talking over a great divide.

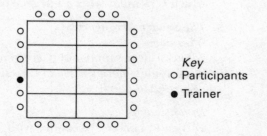

**Figure 4.4** *The 'solid' talking square*

*Disadvantages*
Still inappropriate for the less formal situations.
Requires a large amount of space to be effective.

*Suitable for*
Negotiation skills, team meetings, management role plays.

**Rectangular arrangement**
Although the rectangle layout often utilizes space efficiently it creates a number of difficulties.

*Advantages*
Allows a large number of participants to get round a table.

*Disadvantages*
Heightens visibility difficulties, making it awkward to see round the whole table.

The best positions for eye contact are those participants seated on the short side of the rectangle and consequently these are often seen as

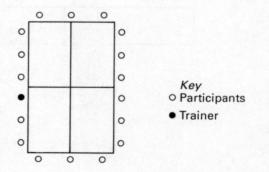

**Figure 4.5** *Rectangular arrangement*

the 'power' positions with commanding control over the whole table. This might produce an 'imbalance' as a result.

*Suitable for*
Board meetings, business games, committee meetings.

### Rows
Unless the rows of desks are also tiered, this layout should be avoided.

*Advantages*
Formality.

*Disadvantages*
Difficult to see anything past the head of the persons in front. Allows less interested parties to hide in the back row.

*Suitable for*
Providing the desks are tiered, the setting can be used for large groups where space is at a premium.

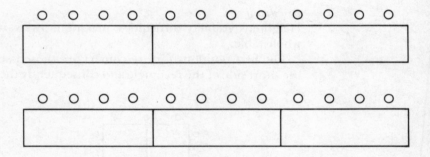

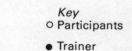

Key
○ Participants

● Trainer

**Figure 4.6** *Rows*

### The classroom arrangement
Classroom style is seen most frequently in schools and examination halls.

*Advantages*
Improves trainer's access and allows instruction to be given on an individual basis.

*Disadvantages*
The association with schools and examinations can create an unnecessary barrier to learning.

*Suitable for*
Individual training, languages, typing, computing, and general keyboard skills.

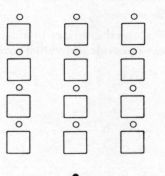

**Figure 4.7** *Classroom*

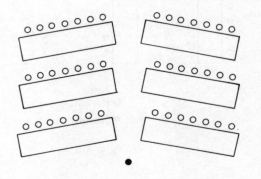

**Figure 4.8** *Chevrons*

### Chevrons
An alternative to the militaristic rows would be to organize the desks diagonally in a chevron or herringbone pattern.

*Advantages*
Improved sight lines provide increased communication between the ranks of tables.
    Creates a sense of individual teams.

*Disadvantages*
Can give rise to competitiveness and sense of 'us and them'.

*Suitable for*
Small team programmes, workshops, team building.

### 'U' and 'V' layouts
Where rectangular tables are used 'U' and 'V' layouts are very popular.

*Advantages*
The open 'U' allows the trainer to move into the group to encourage responses and to provide individual coaching or counselling.

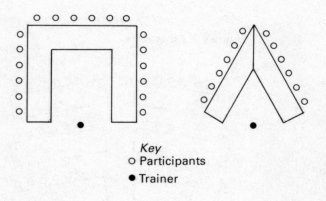

Key
o Participants
● Trainer

**Figure 4.9** *'U' and 'V' styles*

The greatest position or command over the group is seen as the person occupying the middle of the 'V' or 'U' which is no doubt why this set up is popular with trainers.

*Disadvantages*
Best suited to small/medium sized training groups.

*Suitable for*
Most courses but particularly presentation skills.

**Bistro style**
Bistro or cabaret style seating is used extensively in certain programmes and can comprise rectangular or round tables.

*Advantages*
Sets the scene for informal participation.
    Ideal for situations where different tasks are allocated to different tables.

*Disadvantages*
Not appropriate for training requiring overall eye contact as it encourages small cliques to develop.
    May be difficult to control.

*Suitable for*
Workshops, small group work, problem solving.

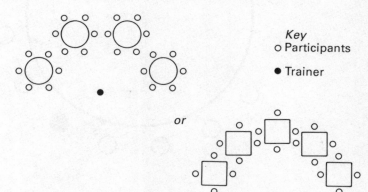

**Figure 4.10** *The 'bistro' style*

### Round tables

The most obvious benefit of round tables are that by their very design there cannot be a head of the table. However, in practice this might be academic because invariably those sitting nearest to any flip chart or visual supports are perceived to be in control.

*Advantages*

Single status.

Excellent sight lines.

High level of involvement.

*Disadvantages*

No obvious leader.

Difficult to find round tables.

Difficult for trainer to circulate.

*Suitable for*

Information sharing, fact finding, problem solving.

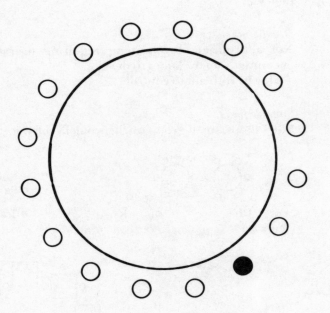

Key
o Participants

● Trainer

**Figure 4.11** *Round tables*

### Seminar seating

The wider availability of seminar seating with arm tablets to write upon has led to a corresponding increase in the popularity of seminars as a training arrangement.

*Advantages*
Provides maximum flexibility.
Chairs can be set up in different designs (see Figure 4.12).

*Disadvantages*
Could be too informal.
Not recommended where considerable written work undertaken.
Awkward for left-handed participants.

*Suitable for*
Highly synergistic forms of training, such as brainstorms, role plays and interpersonal skills.

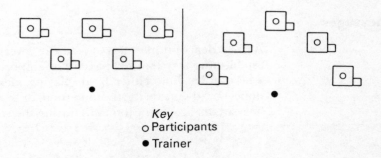

Key
o Participants
● Trainer

**Figure 4.12** *Seminar seating, with arm tablets*

# Lighting

The lighting which is most appropriate for each training course will be dictated by the type of course being undertaken. Where there is a good deal of close-up work the lighting should be greater, while sessions dependent upon the group being relaxed and uninhibited are best carried out in subdued lighting. (It is difficult to run a successful stress programme when the glare from the lighting puts everyone under the spotlight.)

For most purposes the minimum lighting requirement should be 30-50 foot candles (a 'foot candle' being the basic unit of light measurement) increasing to 70 foot candles when detailed work is involved.

To provide greatest flexibility lighting should be both dimmable and directional.

## Location

The location of a venue should be considered very carefully. It should be central enough to be accessible to all participants with the minimum of difficulty.

Even where the course is intended to be a retreat or to make use of natural surroundings for team development, it is still necessary to have good transport facilities and communications.

Where the course is a residential one the group must feel that there is a justifiable reason for making it so and the accommodation facilities must be suitable for the course in question (see Accommodation).

## Messages

A great deal of unnecessary anxiety or interruption can be avoided by establishing a system for passing on important messages to trainees. This can be done either by displaying messages on an appropriate noticeboard outside the training room or by arranging for messages to be read out at specific intervals during the course.

### TRAINER'S TIP

The best time to deliver messages is immediately before any breaks. If an important message is given out on returning from a break the participant is likely to spend time pondering over the reason for a message rather than concentrating on the course material.

To assist with the smooth running of the message system, notify course participants of the name and number of the person to be contacted should a message be necessary and explain that only messages of major importance will be allowed to interrupt the course.

## Noise

There is little point in presenting your material in a lively and informative way unless the group can hear what you are saying.

Floors should be carpeted and there should be sufficient sound-proofing to prevent echoes.

Where possible check the room out in advance. It is surprising the number of training rooms which are located adjacent to the kitchens, overlooking a busy thoroughfare, or above the lift winching machinery.

It is also advisable to ask who will be using any neighbouring rooms and what they are intending to use them for. Booking a Presentation Course next to 'Introduction to the Chain Saw' is a recipe for disaster.

### TRAINER'S TIP

Remember that even with the best sound-proofing many sounds can be generated within the training room. Look out for noisy heaters, air conditioning, or overhead projectors.

## Rubbish Bins

There is often an appalling scarcity of rubbish bins in training rooms and bearing in mind the amount of scrap paper, paper cups, or sweet wrappers that are generated, this should be remedied if the room isn't going to look like a devastation area on completing the course.

## Screens

Where the training produced relies heavily on visual support care should be taken to check that the trainee's view of the screen is unobstructed. If the screen is too close, group members will experience discomfort and fatigue. Too far away and they will experience eye strain and headaches.

The ideal distances depend on the size of the screen in use but as a broad measure the maximum distance from the screen to the last row of seats should not exceed 6 screen widths, while the front row should not be any closer to the screen than two screen widths.

The best viewing area within these parameters would be 3 screen widths across, which would ensure that no one was more than one width to the left or right of the centre line.

As for the height of the screen, this must allow the group to see above the heads without craning their necks or having to look 'round' the person in front.

There are many different types of screen, ranging from flat white to lenticular. Silver screens, for example, prevent interference with the screen image by reflecting back any stray light. This does mean though that it can be difficult to see clearly unless the screen is viewed 'head on'. Beaded fabrics, on the other hand, have a high light return and are also lightweight, which can be an advantage where portability is required.

Whichever screen is chosen make sure that it is durable, kept free from damp and dust and cleaned in accordance with the manufacturer's instructions.

## Sunlight

Everyone appreciates a sunny day but sunlight itself can be a very disruptive influence on training courses. Quite apart from the fact that light reflected off whiteboards and other equipment can make it difficult to focus on the material, it can also cause migraines and eye strain.

As far as circumstances allow take steps to protect trainees from the glare by making use of blinds, curtains or shutters. If you know that the afternoon sun floods into the room make a point of warning people and giving them the option to move.

Check that the sunlight doesn't affect the visibility of slides and other visual support. Often sunlight will blur the definition or lighten the image until it disappears into obscurity.

## Tables

Tables can be both a hindrance and a help. They are a hindrance because they establish barriers between people. Where the need is to overcome obstacles and establish an informal understanding between people as quickly as possible, the layout and existence of tables can be a decisive factor.

Where tables are used these should be of a size and depth which is sufficient for the purpose intended. Allow approximately 30" (76 cms) per person and a depth of 20" (51 cms) for each group member to spread out their materials.

A possible alternative to formal tabling is to use student chairs, or chairs with arm tablets. These are very suitable for situations where there is a need for informality but also for an opportunity to make the occasional notes. They are not suited to situations where there will be extensive writing.

The arm tablets should be approximately 27" (69 cms) from the floor and inclined slightly to allow notes to be taken without unduly straining.

# Temperature

The temperature, like the weather, is one of the factors where you cannot hope to please all of the people all of the time. However, most people find it comfortable between 68 - 76° Fahrenheit (or 20 - 25°C).

When considering the temperature it is important to take into account the amount of electric equipment being used. The more videos, computers and projectors involved the quicker the temperature will start to rise and the higher it will stay.

Other factors which will affect the temperature will be the size of the room, the number of people attending and the activities being undertaken. If the room has a large number of windows the effect could be to turn the room into a fridge first thing in the morning and a greenhouse in the afternoon. To avoid this, check for curtaining or window blinds.

# Toilets

Toilets are an essential comfort factor. The main points to check are that there are adequate facilities for both sexes and that they are sufficiently near the training room. Where disabled or special care groups may be attending courses, additional factors to consider will be accessibility and suitability of equipment (see Disabled).

# Windows

Windows are not merely a method of providing additional light and ventilation for a room, they can also be a major distraction.

Wherever possible the training room should be set up so that the trainees are sitting with their back to any windows. If the windows are behind the trainer the group's attention will be inevitably drawn to what is happening outside.

## TRAINER'S TIP

Sometimes the doors of training rooms have a small glass pane. This should be covered up with paper to prevent people looking in and distracting the trainees. A half inch hole can be cut out to allow interested parties to check whether the room is in use.

See also the 'Checklist' section for a list of accommodation and venue requirements.

# 5 Training Methods

▷            SUMMARY            ◁

This chapter:
- Considers how a training method is selected.
- Highlights six specific training methods (lecture, role play, case studies, 'in' tray exercises, brainstorming and discussions).
- Provides a quick-reference alphabetical list of training methods at the end of the chapter.

## Selecting a Training Method

One of the aspects which must be considered when designing a training course is the way it is intended to convey the information to the group of trainees. There are a variety of different training methods available to choose from and selecting the most appropriate one can make a substantial difference to the reception of your training message and the length of time it is retained after the course is completed.

The important factor to recognize is that there isn't just one way of delivering the material. In the same way that there might be many routes to the same destination, there can be a number of different approaches which will fulfil the training objectives. No one route is the right one, but a particular path might be more effective when all the circumstances are considered.

Some of the variables that will influence the choice of training method selected might include:

| | |
|---|---|
| Course objectives | Equipment needed |
| Time available | Degree of interaction required |
| Participant's level of understanding | Degree of participation expected |
| Any previous experience | Size of group |
| Financial resources available | Facilities available |

It is also worth emphasizing that there is no inviolable rule that states that the trainer should use only one training method for the duration of the course. Using a variety of techniques not only increases the group's attention span but it will frequently reflect the working reality where a combination of different approaches might be needed. If, for example, it would be normal practice to follow up a critical incident with an evaluation of the procedure adopted, then it would make equal good sense to follow up a simulated incident or case study with some form of discussion and assessment.

---

### TRAINER'S TIP

There are essentially three ways in which a trainer can deliver instruction:
1. *Communicating* instruction verbally.
   For example: talks, lectures and discussion.
2. *Demonstrating* the skills or tasks required.
   For example: presentations, demonstrations, and modelling
3. Giving trainees the opportunities for *practising* the skills necessary.
   For example: letter writing, computer programming, office practice.

Any training method selected will comprise one or more of these components – communication, demonstration or practice. It is also important to emphasize that the inclusion of one component doesn't preclude the use of the others.

---

## Methods

The pages that follow contain a cross-section of specific training methods. Each one is sub-divided to include a brief description of the actual method and then this is expanded to provide some background information, useful tips and techniques, and finally the advantages and disadvantages associated wtih that particular approach.

The methods examined comprise:

| | |
|---|---|
| Lectures | 'In' tray |
| Role play | Brainstorming |
| Case study | Discussion |

At the end of the chapter you will find an alphabetical list of training methods with advantages and disadvantages of each.

## Lecture

### Description

In its most common form a lecture is a talk or verbal presentation given by a lecturer, trainer or speaker to an audience.

The object is for the lecturer to convey aspects of his or her knowledge to the group which they are then expected to absorb and retain. The absence of any involvement other than listening by the audience means that the process is essentially a passive one with little or no opportunity for the group to interact.

### Background

It is strange that with all the advances in training systems and computer technology, it is still the lecture which forms the backbone of much of today's training. It is also the instructional method which in practice is the most mis-used.

In many cases the reason for this is the commonly held belief that the person possessing the greatest knowledge of a subject is also the person best equipped to deliver this knowledge to others. Unfortunately expertise in the topic is no indication of a person's ability to present this material in an informative and stimulating way.

### Approach

The best policy to adopt when preparing a talk or lecture, is to be 'an expert on your audience as well as an authority in your subject'.

This approach will help to avoid the lecture becoming a monologue and develop it instead into something which the group can identify with and be involved in. The skills required to do this are mainly those needed to become an accomplished speaker in any area:

1. Ascertain the *needs* of your audience.

   Find out in advance exactly what it is that the group *needs* to know. This is not as easy to achieve in practice as it might first seem. This is because even though reference is made throughout this book to the 'group' or an 'audience' in reality there may be little homogeneity. There is only a collection of individuals brought together for a common purpose but all retaining their own unique and individual expectations, attitudes and requirements.

   It is part of the trainer's function to discover the areas where

65

these interests overlap and to develop the training course in a way that is best suited to satisfy these requirements.

2. Highlight the benefits

Merely ascertaining what the group *needs* to know will not ensure that on completing the course the group will have grasped these factors. People only learn when they are convinced that there is some benefit in doing so. It is therefore vital to provide this motivation by clearly demonstrating the advantages to be gained from participating in the training.

These rewards aren't purely monetary but extend to promotional opportunities, job satisfaction and greater recognition, all of which might accompany the acquisition of new skills and knowledge.

3. Check the level of understanding

No matter how great the need and desire to learn, people cannot learn what they can't understand.

To check understanding means that the trainer must take account of two elements. First, he or she must be able to gauge the *level of knowledge* within the group. Where do they fit in on the scale between interested novices and acknowledged authorities? The conclusion you reach will dictate the degree of complexity incorporated in your lecture.

If you aim too low you risk patronising your audience and reducing involvement still further. If you miscalculate and make the course too advanced you are likely to undermine confidence, alienate the group and increase boredom. The balance, as always, is a delicate one.

Second, the trainer must consider the *level of comprehension* of the group. Wherever possible, technical terms and jargon should be eliminated. In those situations where technical phrases are unavoidable, a clear explanation of what they mean should be given. Training is about advancing understanding, not making people feel inadequate for any lack of understanding. Improved understanding can be further enhanced by adhering to the following guidelines:

– Structure your lecture

Preparation time is never wasted. A few minutes spent thinking about the sequence of delivery beforehand can go a considerable way to improving retention afterwards. The information presented should follow a natural sequence which is apparent to everyone. If the process in question is complicated take the group through it one step at a time.

If their understanding would be increased by some background knowledge, start by examining the topic from an historical basis. Improve the rate of absorption by breaking the information into easily assimilable portions.

## TRAINER'S TIP

A simple method of structuring a lecture is to divide it into three categories:
- Commencement (or Introduction)
- Core
- Conclusion

incorporating the information set out below:

Commencement (Introduction):
>Who you are.
>Why you are here.
>Your authority for addressing the group.
>The objectives of the presentation.
>The relevance of the topic to the group.
>Any benefits arising as a consequence.
>Proposed structure.
>Any technical definitions.
>Assumed knowledge, background or historical information.

Core:
>Key points discussed sequentially.

Conclusion:
>Review of information covered.
>Re-emphasis of main messages or learning points.
>Summation linking to the future.

— Reinforce your message
- Tell the group what you are going to tell them.
- Then tell them.
- Then tell them what you told them.

This repetition will be perfectly acceptable and will clarify and re-emphasize the learning points.

— Aid concentration

Keep your presentation within the confines of the audience's concentration span. Twenty minutes is generally regarded as the optimum attention span, but this can be extended to forty minutes in certain circumstances by including a change of style, pace or delivery after a twenty minute period. An example of this might be stopping for a period of questioning, or an opportunity to distribute and consider handouts.

### Tips and techniques

Because lecturing is by its very nature a non-participative training method, careful thought has to be given to developing techniques which make maximum use of the opportunities for involvement.

1. Material

   Considerable thought should be given to the nature and order of the material used. If your audience is to be receptive to your message the material should be stimulating and thought provoking. A continuous stream of facts and figures is unlikely to be a challenge to anyone's senses. So that a weak structure would be:

   Introduction
   Fact
   Fact
   Fact
   Data
   Conclusion

   A far more dynamic approach would be to select material which would enthral or inspire the group. A structure reflecting this might be:

   Introduction (unusual/surprising)
   Relevant Quote/ little known fact
   Fact
   Real life illustration/anecdote
   Fact
   Stimulating conclusion

2. Make it memorable

   An additional benefit of selecting your material carefully is that it will draw a response from the group and will ensure that your training message is remembered.

   The mundane is soon forgotten, but issues which are emotive or provocative will be the source of informative debate long after the lecture has been forgotten. This doesn't mean that your material should be insensitive or controversial just for the sake of it. However, if there are areas where experts disagree or counter arguments to the popular views exist these should be provided too.

3. Deliver it dynamically

   Delivering information *dynamically* isn't the same as delivering the information *dramatically*.

Emphasize the positive attributes rather than the negative and use language that reinforces this. All that is required is that information is given in a way that reflects your enthusiasm for the topic and will intrigue your audience.

Phrases like:
- 'This is an interesting issue . . .'
- 'I'm sure that many of you have wondered . . .'
- 'One of the most exciting discoveries . . .'

all help the group to feel that they are sharing the experience with the lecturer.

While expressions like:
- 'I don't suppose . . .'
- 'If you were able to . . .'

are likely to alienate the group and leave them feeling deflated.

4. Use questions

One of the simplest and most effective means of involving a group is to use rhetorical questions. These are questions which are asked in order to promote thought rather than elicit verbal response. Examples of this are:
- 'Who hasn't at some time . . .'
- 'Don't you ever wish . . .'
- 'Isn't it funny how . . .'

The effectiveness of these questions are that they start the group thinking about what their reaction *would* be even though they might not have the chance in reality to voice this.

It is also worth noting that rhetorical questions are not the only form of questioning possible during a lecture. There is nothing preventing any speaker from stopping a talk at any point and introducing a short question and answer session. While many speakers may indicate directly or indirectly that they should not be interrupted there is no rule which makes this sacrosanct, and a few well-timed questions can do a lot to lift flagging attention and enhance participation. (In any event, the group should certainly be given an opportunity to raise any burning issues they might have even if this means providing a few minutes for questions at the end of the session.)

5. Visual Support

The final technique available to the speaker as a means of developing involvement, is to reinforce any learning points with appropriate visual support. Using slides, transparencies or flip charts can add a dimension which cannot fail to evoke a response just by stimulating the senses.

*Advantages of the lecture method*

1. Ideal for large groups

Speaking to large numbers of people can be a complicated and cumbersome process. Lecturing provides the only viable means of communicating with a large group of people quickly and efficiently. The only factors limiting the size of the audience for a lecture are the capacity of the venue and the ability to hear what is being said.

2. Economical

The ability to present a lecture to a large group of people also makes this a very economical method of instruction. It is considerably more cost effective to deliver a lecture to 50 people than to run five training sessions for ten people at a time.

3. Material is covered in a structured manner

The way that a lecture is prepared ensures that to some extent there will always be some order or logical sequencing of material. The more logical the material the easier the information will be understood and assimilated.

4. Control of material

One of the effects of a logical structure is that it becomes possible to control the material presented and to predict with some certainty what aspects of the subject will be covered and what issues will not. This ability means that the trainer can determine in advance what points he or she wants to stress, and in which order, without fear of being side-tracked or overlooked.

5. Greater control of time

Lecturing also provides greater control over time. Although it will not be possible to assess any question and answer session following on from the lecture, it should be possible with practice to calculate the time that the actual lecture will take.

*Disadvantages of the lecture method*

1. Passive approach

The biggest single disadvantage of using lectures as a method of instruction is that they involve their audience to such a minimal degree. This can be counteracted by following the lecture by a question and answer session.

2. No feedback

One of the effects of the lack of interaction is that it becomes difficult to gauge how much the audience has understood and absorbed.

### 3. Demanding

The capabilities of the trainer can have a more profound effect on the success or failure of the lecture than might be the case where other methods are used.

If the trainer is accomplished, the lecture will be stimulating, thought provoking and absorbing. If the trainer is weak, the consequence will be lack of attention, distraction and low retention. The process is therefore a challenging one and calls for a level of concentration both on the trainer's part and on the part of the audience.

*Application*

Most topics can be made the subject of a lecture or talk. However, lectures should be avoided where the group requires some form of activity, or where learning is achieved by sharing experiences.

## Role Plays

*Description*

Role play is a means of extending trainees' experience by presenting them with a commonly encountered situation and asking them to place themselves in the position of the parties involved (the role) and then act out the way in which the circumstances might reach an appropriate conclusion (the play).

*Approach*

To gain the maximum benefit from role play as a teaching method it is essential that the incidents selected for enactment are as realistic as the situation allows. Time should be taken to prepare an outline brief of the personalities involved and to ensure that the circumstances closely reflect those encountered in the working environment.

The brief should be sufficiently detailed to make clear the issues involved but sufficiently flexible to allow the individual to develop the role in accordance with his or her own interpretation of how matters might be handled.

The object of the exercise is for the group to portray the behaviour that they believe would be demonstrated by the persons in the roles that they have been allotted. It should be emphasized that it is this *behaviour* which will be the foundation of any later discussion and not the *acting* talents of those taking part. The group should be looking at the content and process of any scenario. This can be reinforced by asking those who are not involved to assume the role of observers and to note down the effects and implications of the behaviour displayed.

Observation can be further enhanced by using a video camera to record the role play and then to use this to provide group feedback or individual counselling as desired.

### Tips and techniques
1. Schedule carefully
Used correctly, role play can provide an invaluable learning experience for participants. The exercise should be timetabled towards the middle of the course to allow the group to overcome any initial inhibitions that they might have.
2. Use selectively
The effectiveness of role play can be attributed in part to the participative nature and novelty of the exercise. This means that role play should be used with discretion. If over-used its value can decline rapidly.
3. Keep groups small
Reference has already been made to overcoming inhibitions and this can be assisted by ensuring that the group size doesn't exceed ten members. This will help to create the informal and relaxed atmosphere necessary for the exercise to succeed.

Where the numbers attending are likely to exceed ten, there are still opportunities to use role play as part of the training programme. Large groups can be broken down into smaller syndicates, each with their own observer, set of role plays and instructions asking them to reassemble at a given time to discuss their findings with the whole group.
4. Use role play creatively
There is no reason why role play should be viewed in isolation. The best approach is to follow a session of theoretical input with an opportunity to link this with a practical role play applying the principles discussed.

Where there is some benefit to be gained by all trainees experiencing a particular situation, a multiple role play could be undertaken by sub-dividing the group and each smaller unit enacting the scenario simultaneously.

Alternatively, a greater appreciation of the problems and perspective of other people can be achieved, by a reverse role play. This is where, at a certain point in the proceedings, the two parties to the role play are asked to swop (or reverse) roles and to present a case from the opposite point of view and to put a case which often will contradict their normal standpoint.

*Advantages of role play*

1. Memorable

'Learning by doing' is one of the most effective means of learning and experiences gained first-hand are remembered clearly and for longer.

2. Enjoyable

In most cases role play offers a relatively painless and enjoyable way of assimilating knowledge.

3. Creates understanding

The way in which a role play allows participants to discover how they would feel when faced with certain situations can be a powerful learning tool and can develop an appreciation of others' predicaments which would be hard to provide in any other way.

4. Low risk environment

Although using role play can involve an element of high risk, this has more to do with the way that the *group* might react than the effect of the role play on others. Role play gives the trainee a chance to simulate or rehearse a variety of behaviours, free of the dangers that experimenting with approaches might produce if carried out in the normal working environment.

*Disadvantages of role play*

1. Can be artificial

The essence of a successful role play exercise is to make the situations as credible as circumstances permit. If the group feel that the scenario is unrealistic or that it fails to take account of current working practices, the value will be lost and the learning points dismissed.

2. Taken frivolously

If the objectives of the exercise are not fully explained and emphasis is not given to the behaviour shown (and not dramatic skills) then there is a danger of role play being viewed as a 'bit of fun'. Establishing the serious purpose of the exercise doesn't prevent people from enjoying it providing any pleasure is derived from identification with the situation and the outcome, rather than the humorous way it is portrayed.

3. Element of risk

As with any highly participative training method there is always an element of risk. Role playing can only work if the group is prepared to join in. If group members feel concerned about losing prestige in front of colleagues or are embarrassed by the process, the exercise cannot work. This makes it even more crucial that the exercise is carefully controlled.

The size of the group should not be so large that any member should feel intimidated. It should only be undertaken when the group has relaxed and self-esteem is no longer of paramount importance.

*Applications*

Role play is most frequently associated with interpersonal skills such as interviewing, negotiation, appraisal, selling and even training itself. However, with a bit of forethought there is no logical reason why the process should not be extended to cover any training situation.

## Case Study

*Description*

The use of case studies as a means of training have become increasingly popular in recent years. In most case studies the trainees will be presented with a record of a set of circumstances which might be based on an actual event or an imaginary situation.

*Approach:*

There are three main categories of case study:

1. Those asking the trainee to diagnose a particular problem.
2. Those which identify the problem or problems but require the trainee to recommend methods of resolving these difficulties.
3. Those case studies which provide both the problem and the solution but ask the group to explain why this action was taken and the implications this might have.

Once the appropriate category has been selected it is possible to decide whether the case study will involve one issue or a series of issues for the group to resolve.

The complexity of the issues will also dictate whether the case study is incorporated into the training programme as a short 30–60 minute exercise or a more lengthy undertaking. In more advanced situations the course might even be built around the case study itself and last several days.

In each of these examples the learning element will be achieved by providing information on an issue or series of issues. This information might be in documentary form, (such as a report) or it could be communicated through oral or visual means (such as a video or slide presentation). Once the group has been provided with the raw data to examine, the process of analysis can begin and any further details furnished.

The trainer can maintain control by:
– extending or reducing the time constraints.

- laying down certain parameters within which the group must operate, e.g. 'no further information need be sought' or 'any additional research must be undertaken by the group'.
- limiting or expanding the detail required from the group on completion, e.g. full report, main recommendations, presentation, etc.
- increasing or reducing the pressure by encouraging competition between groups, introducing unexpected events, etc.

At the end of the exercise the group should be required to reconvene to discuss the reasons for their actions and to identify the learning experiences they have gained.

### Tips and techniques

1. Select suitable material

The material selected for inclusion in the case study must reflect issues which trainees might face in reality. It should contain enough detail for the group to feel conversant with all the facts without providing so much that the participants feel overwhelmed. Additional information can always be provided subsequently. (This can either happen automatically or be dependent on the group requesting further data.)

2. Allow for alternatives

The issue chosen should be one which is wide enough to take account of the different areas of specialism of the participants and allow for a variety of different approaches. Problems which provide for only one definitive 'right' answer are therefore less effective.

3. Keep the groups small

The larger the group, the more cumbersome and unwieldy the exercise can become. To obtain the optimum results from the case study, limit the group size to a maximum of ten people. If larger groups are inevitable, consider breaking the groups into small syndicates each looking at the different aspects of the same problem. Alternatively inject an element of competition by forming groups into 'companies' with the task of resolving the problem before their competitors.

### Advantages of case study

1. Adds realism

Using case studies as part of a training course can offset the more theoretical aspects of the course by introducing some real issues for the group to resolve.

2. Minimizes pressure

Case studies provide a unique opportunity to examine complex or emotive issues in a detached manner away from the pressures which would normally be associated with the actual event. This permits learning to take place without the concern for the implications which might arise if the decision is incorrect.

3. Encourages communication

The importance of discussing problems and proposed solutions fully is quickly appreciated during the exercise.

*Disadvantages of case study*

1. Could mislead

While the capacity to read, analyse and review each step taken towards a solution is one of the great benefits of the case study method, it is also one of its drawbacks too. It is highly unlikely that faced with a similar problem in the workplace, a trainee would have the time, knowledge, and lack of pressure to resolve the situation in quite the same way. This fact must be made clear to trainees to avoid their becoming disillusioned back in their working environment.

2. Inconclusive

Where pressure of time prevents a group making any recommendations this is likely to result in a general feeling of dissatisfaction.

3. Credibility

The need for realism is a constant factor in any training exercise and case studies are no exception. The brief must be one that the group can identify with and respond to. It must follow the same pattern and be subject to the same policies and restraints that they will find in practice.

*Applications*

Suitable for small groups or larger groups (if divided into syndicates). Case studies have the greatest effect on areas requiring analytical abilities. This includes problem-solving, decision-making, negotiation, and industrial relations. Other areas include management and supervisory skills, sales and administration.

## 'In' Tray

*Description*

'In' tray exercises are sometimes known as 'In' basket exercises and consist of a paper-handling simulation based on the contents of a typical company worker's 'In' tray. The object of the exercise is for the trainee involved to be projected into the position of the person responsible for dealing with the 'In' tray items and then to resolve all the work it contains. On completion of the exercise the trainee's progress is reviewed.

*Approach*

'In' tray exercises are generally used in two situations. First, as a diagnostic tool to discover how the group member would handle the work outstanding in the tray. Second, as an evaluative method to assess how the trainee would put into effect the skills learnt on the training course.

In the first situation each course member will be given a series of items to sort through and action would be taken on these in the way that the trainee felt appropriate.

The exercise would be carried out independently and the final stage will be to reconvene as a group to review the decisions or action taken and to assess their effectiveness.

Where the 'In' tray is used as an evaluative method the approach is similar. The items in the 'In' tray – files, letters, and memoranda – are reviewed individually and action taken by the person involved. The main difference lies in the fact that prior to undertaking the task the trainee will be given advice on the best means of dealing with the work problems that the tray highlights. The success of the trainee will be judged on his or her ability to apply these criteria in handling the work in the exercise.

It is important to emphasize that providing the feedback at the end of the exercise is an essential ingredient in the learning process and adequate time should be provided to do this.

### Tips and techniques
1.  Match content to objectives
The files, letters or other items used as the basis of the exercise should reflect the nature of the work typically carried out by those attending and it should illustrate the course objectives. If, for example, the purpose of the course is to manage stress successfully, then the contents of the 'In' tray must involve meeting tight deadlines and require resolutions in 40 minutes, before the trainee will be 'called away to a meeting' to discuss his progress.

Alternatively, if the objective of the course is to use time more effectively, the amount of work requiring action should exceed the time available. This will result in the trainee having to prioritize the work in order to satisfy the more urgent tasks.

2.  Avoid delegation
The instructions should make it clear that the group members are required to implement the action required and not just analyse the steps they would take if faced with the problem. So that in a time-management course it will not be acceptable to state 'delegate work to office junior', nor will it be sufficient on a letter-writing course to include 'respond to letter from M. Curtis'. Instead the participants

must take the necessary steps to deal with the problem and to draft the letter in reply.

3. Provide variety

The items selected for the 'In' tray should seek to identify a range of skills needed to perform the job. As far as possible each item should highlight a different facet or demonstrate a different learning point.

*Advantages of 'in-tray'*

1. Real life problems

The essence of any good training is to ensure that it accurately reflects the working environment. A well-prepared 'In' Tray exercise can provide one of the closest simulations achievable, allowing actual working examples to be used as the foundation for group analysis.

2. Monitor progress

Depending on what stage in the course the 'In' tray exercise is undertaken, the process will highlight either the knowledge of the group members at the beginning of the course or the level of comprehension at the programme's end. In either case it will be possible to gain an accurate insight into the progress of training.

3. Practical

The very nature of the exercise means that trainees can see that the training is not just participative but immensely practical and directly applicable to the work they do.

4. Alters attitudes

'In' tray exercises also develop the participant's approach to working situations. For example, as a consequence of discussion and analysis the trainees' perception of priorities or the needs of the customer will be amended.

5. Flexible numbers

The only limitations to the numbers of trainees taking part in an 'In' tray exercise, are those caused by difficulties in providing individual feedback. This can be easily overcome by providing feedback on a group basis or, where large numbers are involved, encouraging one group to provide a critique of another.

*Disadvantages of 'in-tray'*

1. Improbability

The situations encountered in going through the 'In' tray's contents must be viewed by the trainees as a reasonable representation of the work they would expect to see. If the practical element is lost so is the value of the exercise.

2. Trainer's preferences

It is inevitable when dealing with some items in an 'In' tray that the trainer's own style of dealing with certain problems will be reflected in the approach that is advocated. If this style doesn't correspond with the working habits of the trainees this might make the trainee less receptive to some of the more fundamental learning points.

*Applications*
Useful to demonstrate effective problem-solving or decision-making, time management, elementary writing skills, customer complaints, management and supervisory training.

# Brainstorming

*Description*
Although its title is a little disconcerting, brainstorming is essentially a loosely structured form of discussion. Its main function is to provide a practical means of generating ideas without participants becoming embroiled in unproductive analysis.

*Approach*
Brainstorming is dependent for its success on two main tenets. The first one is founded in synergistic theory, that a group can produce more high quality ideas by working together than the same people would produce working independently. This is because the greater degree of interaction produces cross-fertilization, so that an idea which on its own might be dismissed as impractical will result in someone else adapting, adopting or improving it to provide a more feasible approach.

The second belief is that if a group is to produce ideas it is imperative that creative thinking isn't inhibited by subjecting these ideas to an evaluation too early on.

Creative thought passes through three stages:
- The generation of the idea.
- The evaluation or analysis of that idea.
- The application of the idea to the chosen situation.

If others sit in judgement after each idea is proposed then 'analysis paralysis' sets in and the flow of ideas dry up. Creative thought can only be stimulated in an environment where judgement is postponed until *after* all the possible solutions have been provided.

This has resulted in the development of a set of six ground rules for running a brainstorming session.

1. No criticism

The free flow of ideas can only take place when there is no fear of being criticized. Criticism in this context is given a wide interpretation, so that this will clearly preclude an outright attack on a proposal, but it also extends to cover indirect ridiculing of someone's idea or being very patronizing about it.

It is also important *not* to imply that an idea has no merit by ignoring any contribution or by betraying cynicism through such non-verbal gestures as a dismissive shrug or raised eyebrows.

2. Encourage ideas

In order to ensure that there are enough ideas for cross-fertilization to take place the group must feel that their contributions are valued. The emphasis should be on the quantity of suggestions and *not* the quality. There will be sufficient opportunity at the evaluation stage for individuals to voice their feelings about any particular suggestion.

3. Equal participation

It follows that if everyone should feel that their suggestion is worthy of consideration then everyone should be entitled to put forward their ideas. The fairest way to prevent one or two more dominant group members from monopolizing the group is to establish a system where each person is asked for a contribution in turn. This might make the process more regimented but this is more than compensated for by the involvement of the whole group.

If a member of the group is unable to make a suggestion at any point this should be indicated by the individual concerned and this should be accepted without comment and the process continued. (It is quite likely that while no idea springs to mind this time round, subsequent recommendations might trigger a thought for next time.)

4. Free association

In order to gain the maximum number of suggestions there shouldn't be any boundaries on what is suggested. Any idea (no matter how outrageous or far fetched it might seem) is worthy of consideration. The logic behind this is that invariably an idea which seems completely impractical could provide the basis of a notion in somebody else's mind.

5. Record all ideas

It isn't just the suggestions which are important but also the opportunity to reflect on them in the hope of inspiring further ideas.

In order to allow this to happen *all* the ideas should be recorded on a flip chart, whiteboard, etc., and in the same words given by the proposer. The reason for this is that to require further clarification can interrupt the flow of thought and be viewed by some group members as seeking justification before acceptance.

6. Allow time to incubate

Once the ideas have been set down there should be some time – an hour, day, week or month to contemplate these suggestions and consider any alternative approaches or any additions to the list.

When running a brainstorming session it is essential that these ground rules are communicated to the group and adhered to throughout the process. To facilitate this, it is advisable to write the rules up and display them prominently in front of the group before brainstorming begins.

---

## TRAINER'S TIP

Having displayed the rules prominently, outline the process to the group. This should begin with an explanation of the reasons for brainstorming and what it is that the exercise is seeking to achieve: 'The aim of this brainstorming session is to think of ways to make employees more safety conscious.' Encapsulate this objective in a word or sentence and place this as the heading of any flip chart, whiteboard or transparency. Then introduce the procedure to the group highlighting the ground rules and expanding them where necessary.

It is also useful to re-state that there will be an opportunity to voice any opinions on any proposal at a later stage but the brainstorming process is purely for generating ideas, *not* for evaluating them.

If there are time constraints it might be worthwhile mentioning these so that the group is aware that they only have 20 minutes for this stage of the procedure.

---

*Advantages of brainstorming*

1. Encourages creativity

It is often suggested that creativity is not something which can be instructed and that ideas do not lend themselves easily to a formalized approach. Brainstorming provides one of the few means of generating ideas in a structured way. In fact, it is the very existence of these ground rules which enable brainstorming to work so effectively.

2. Overcomes limited thinking

The process of using other ideas to stimulate your own creativity results in a wider range of suggestions than an individual would have produced if left to his or her own devices. There is also less chance of overlooking the obvious or dismissing an idea as unworkable when there is a degree of collective input.

3. Simplicity

Brainstorming is a technique which is easy to understand and easy to carry out. It requires no hi-tech equipment or advanced training and the results can quickly be assessed.

*Disadvantages of brainstorming*

1. Misleading title

One of the biggest obstacles to the popularity of brainstorming as an instructional method arises from the association it seems to evoke in others. Brainstorming seems to have connotations of mental disturbance or of brainwashing; neither of which are viewed with a great deal of relish by those invited to take part. This can be overcome by acknowledging the anxiety that the title might produce and explaining its less sinister meaning.

2. Highly participative

The highly participative nature of brainstorming is both an advantage and a disadvantage. The advantages of greater involvement are self-explanatory but the disadvantages stem from the reliance the process places on the individuals involved. Brainstorming can only work when the group feel that they have ideas to contribute. If no one is prepared to make suggestions the group will spend the time sitting in stony and embarrassed silence.

3. Incomplete process

Reference has already been made to the fact that brainstorming is only a stage in the problem-solving process. Generating ideas, solutions or recommendations may be very satisfying, but the real rewards are derived from seeing these ideas put into practice. This means that the trainer must stress that actions speak louder than words and that once a solution or idea has been agreed upon it must be put into effect.

*Applications*

Brainstorming is useful for problem-solving, decision-making, and creative thinking. It develops listening skills and provides a useful vehicle for team building.

## Discussion

*Description*

A free verbal exchange of knowledge, ideas or opinions between trainer and trainees.

*Approach*

A discussion for instructional purposes can be differentiated from a social conversation by the fact that a conversation usually covers a range of topics and has no boundaries or structure. Discussions on the other hand, tend to be limited to one aspect or topic and have a degree of order about them. As it is important that everyone should air their views and consider those of others, interruptions become less acceptable.

Discussions need also to be distinguished from *open forum* which as a general rule involve topics of a more contentious nature and provide an opportunity to hear and debate all sides of an issue. Although in many cases a discussion might also involve an emotive area this is not automatically the situation and it is possible for a discussion to take place where everyone is in agreement.

In order to hold an effective discussion it is necessary for the participants to possess a measure of knowledge. This knowledge might be acquired through instruction or experiences gained prior to the course or by information provided on the course itself. So that, for example, by demonstrating a new process to the group it will be possible for a discussion to take place about the difficulties or dangers that they perceive in carrying out the procedure for themselves.

### Tips and techniques
1. Timing and preparation

   As it is the presence of a structured approach that sets a discussion apart from a simple conversation, it is imperative the time is spent on preparing the path that the discussion will take.

   The first step should be to consider what aspects of the chosen topic can be discussed in the time available. There should be sufficient time allocated to do justice to the issues without allowing so much time that the group feel that the ground is being covered *ad nauseam*.

   Any limitations on time should be clearly stated at the start and ideally there should be enough pressure on the group to add an element of urgency to the discussion. This will ensure that matters do not become monotonous and where necessary a conclusion is reached.

2. Planning

   It isn't possible to consider all aspects of a discussion in advance but it is possible to prepare a rough outline to the topic. This outline should:

– Introduce the topic and people involved.
– Establish any parameters to the discussion. What areas will be included and what aspects cannot be.
– Set out the purpose of the discussion. Is it to reach some form of consensus, make recommendations or merely examine the subject from all aspects?

– Provide any background information which can set the topic in context.

– Include a number of basic questions to get the discussion under way and to provide direction and impetus should it begin to flag.

---

## TRAINER'S TIP

Where the training style used is facilitative, the trainer can make the establishment of a plan by the group an integral part of the training itself.

---

3. Create the right environment

Discussion thrives best in an atmosphere which is relaxed and uninhibited. It is important that the group should be able to establish eye contact easily with everyone in the room and that the numbers participating are kept to a minimum. It is difficult to retain an air of informality with forty people around a conference table.

4. Trainer's function

The role of the trainer in any discussion is more akin to that of a facilitator. He or she must ease the group into a discussion by selecting opening questions which will encourage debate without putting people on the defensive from the outset.

Once an exchange has begun the trainer must ensure that no *one* person monopolizes the discussion and that everyone who wishes to make a contribution has a fair opportunity to do so.

Where any comment is ambiguous or vague the trainer may seek clarification from the speaker on behalf of the group or explore points which might have been overlooked or touched upon briefly. It is not necessarily the responsibility of the trainer to evaluate the contributions made by the group but he or she must ensure that any points are relevant and prevent the group from becoming bogged down or side-tracked.

At the end of the discussion or the expiry of the time, the trainer should summarize any points made by the group and accurately reflect any conclusions which might have been reached.

### Advantages of discussion

1. Monitors understanding

Discussion provides a reliable indicator of how well the group understands the key issues involved without the need for a more formal assessment. It also affords the individuals in the group the chance to test their own understanding and beliefs by subjecting them to scrutiny.

2. Gains commitment

   Although lecturing is often a more economical method of communicating with a group of people, discussion can be a good deal more efficient in the long term. This is particularly true where the material being communicated runs contrary to the attitudes of some of the group or involves unpleasant or disagreeable issues. Those who find it difficult to reconcile these ideas are far more likely to be persuaded by discussion than convinced by the impact of a lecture.

3. Interactive

   Discussions are potentially highly participative. It is conceivable that some people might not wish to join in a discussion but if the group, topic and questions are chosen with care it becomes very difficult not to make some contribution to the deliberations.

*Disadvantages of discussion*

1. Deviating from the topic

   The single greatest danger of using discussion as an instructional method is the ease with which it is possible to stray away from the subject. Emphasizing the object, topic and parameters at the beginning of the discussion can help to keep the group on course.

2. Dependent on the group

   The quality of the discussion is very reliant upon the depth of knowledge or experience possessed by the individual group members. It is for this reason that attention should be given to the balance of the group to ensure that there is a spectrum of opinion and backgrounds represented.

3. Entrenchment

   Even though discussion undoubtedly provides the greatest chance of convincing someone to see things from another perspective, it is also possible that if a group member believes his views are under threat his beliefs might become more entrenched.

*Applications*

Discussion is suitable for situations where an exchange of knowledge, beliefs or opinions can provide a helpful insight to others. Other applications include behavioural change programmes, interpersonal skills and the provision of feedback.

| Method* | Participation level | Group size |
|---|---|---|
| Action Maze | High | Small groups or Syndicates |
| Assignments | Low | 15–30 |
| Brainstorming | High | Up to 10 |
| Briefing Groups | Medium | Up to 20 |
| Buzz Groups | Medium | Each group 10 maximum |
| Case Study | High | 10 maximum |
| Clinic | High | 1–8 |
| Debate | High | Unlimited |
| Demonstrations | Low/High | 10–20 |
| Discussion | Medium | 20 maximum |
| Fishbowl | High | 10–12 |
| Incident Process | High | 10 maximum |
| 'In' Tray | High | Small syndicates |
| Games | Medium/High | Varies |
| Lecture | Low | Unlimited |
| Programmed instruction | High | Unlimited |
| Role playing | High | 6–8 |
| Seminar | Medium | 10–20 |
| Sensitivity training | High | 8 maximum |
| Talk | Medium | 12–20 |
| Trips | Medium | 20 approximately |
| Workshops | Medium/High | 20 maximum |

**Table 5.1** *Alphabetical catalogue of training methods*
* See also Table 5.2 for definitions.

| | Description | Advantages | Disadvantages | Applications | Participation level | Group size |
|---|---|---|---|---|---|---|
| ACTION MAZE | Similar to a case study the action maze uses a printed description of a situation to guide the group through to a pre-determined conclusion. At set stages participants are provided with a choice of options and the consequnces which follow will be determined according to the alternatives they have selected. In this way trainees can discover for themselves the soundest approach and the implications of their decisions. | • Groups learn at their own pace<br><br>• Stimulating process | • Time consuming<br><br>• Difficult to produce<br><br>• Those who make incorrect decisions learn the most | Problem-solving<br><br>Decision-making<br><br>Managerial skills<br><br>Supervisory skills | High | Small groups or syndicates |
| ASSIGNMENTS | Usually an exercise requiring members to read a quantity of information and to prepare either written or verbal answers to a series of questions. Can be made more productive by linking with other methods such as discussion. | • Paced by individual<br><br>• Provides feedback of trainee's progress and abilities. | • Passive nature<br><br>• Requires self-motivation | Comprehension<br><br>Writing skills<br><br>Question handling<br><br>Decision making | Low | 15–30 |
| BRAIN-STORMING | Means of generating a quantity of highly creative ideas by a group who make suggestions for later evaluation (See 'Training Methods' for more details) | • Simple and effective procedure<br><br>• Interactive | • Misleading title | Problem diagnosis<br><br>Team building<br><br>Creative thinking | High | Up to 10 |
| BRIEFING GROUPS | Trainer or panel of experts provide the salient facts or a 'brief' on a given topic which then forms the basis for a question and answer session | • Fast pace<br><br>• Simple process | • Too short to be informative<br><br>• Success depends on quality of trainee | Fact finding<br><br>Problem solving | Medium | Up to 20 |
| BUSINESS GAMES (see 'GAMES') | | | | | | |

**Table 5.2** *Summary of training methods (continued overleaf)*

| | Description | Advantages | Disadvantages | Applications | Participation level | Group size |
|---|---|---|---|---|---|---|
| **BUZZ GROUPS** (see also called Breakout Groups Discussion Groups) | Opportunity following lecture to break into smaller groups to discuss issues and then relay views, opinions, questions or conclusions back through the group leader to the whole audience. | • Makes lecture more meaningful<br><br>• Provides feedback<br><br>• Reinforces learning | • Time consuming<br><br>• Requires direction | Large conferences<br><br>Change workshops<br><br>Management programmes | Medium | Each group 10 maximum |
| **CASE STUDY** | Group presented with factual information based on a real situation and asked to discuss the problems, analyse the issues and provide recommendations. (See 'Training Methods' for more details) | • Simulates working reality<br><br>• Risk free exercise | • Time consuming to prepare<br><br>• If not topical loses credibility | Management development<br><br>Decision-making<br><br>Supervisory skills<br><br>Individual relations | High | 10 maximum |
| **CLINIC** | Individual or group training designed to allow groups to discuss and overcome any problems relating to a specified performance area. | • Group decide issue examined<br><br>• Transferable training | • Can be costly<br><br>• Small groups only | Manual skills<br><br>Mechanical ability<br><br>Operating systems<br><br>Customer relations | High | 1–8 |
| **DEBATE** | Verbal exchange between factions holding opposing views with the aim of reaching some conclusions | • Adds vitality<br><br>• Interactive | • Learning dependent on group's knowledge<br><br>• Time consuming<br><br>• Often inconclusive | Active listening<br><br>Presentation skills<br><br>Communication<br><br>Non-verbal behaviour | High | Unlimited |
| **DEMONSTRA-TIONS (and DISPLAYS** | Method of telling and/or showing a group the best approach to handling a given set of circumstances or procedures.<br><br>Participation can be increased by allowing trainees an opportunity to perform the skills under similar conditions | • Highly practical<br><br>• Directly applicable | • Time constraints<br><br>• Individual counselling required | Developing manual skills<br><br>Introducing or improving processes, procedures or systems | Low/high | 10–20 |

**Table 5.2** (*continued*)

| | Description | Advantages | Disadvantages | Applications | Participation level | Group size |
|---|---|---|---|---|---|---|
| **DISCUSSION GROUP** | Formalized verbal exchange between trainee, trainer and the whole group (see 'Training Methods' for more details) | • Instant feedback<br><br>• Develops ideas | • Quality of learning dependent on group's knowledge | Attitudinal change<br><br>Communication skills<br><br>Creative thinking | Medium | 20 max. |
| **FISHBOWL** | Means of studying group behaviour by dividing into teams. One team undertaking a task or discussion while the second team observes and notes the process. The results are then discussed before the roles are reversed. | • Provides useful insight<br><br>• Develops feedback techniques' | • Can be unsettling<br><br>• Element of risk<br><br>• Tight controls needed' | Development programmes<br><br>Inter personal skills<br><br>Decision-making' | High | 10–12 |
| **GAMES (Business Games, Management Games)** | The form depends on the game or exercise in question. They generally involve an element of competion or change. In many cases the group are allotted a role in a created 'Company' and provided with data to run the company for a period of time or for the duration of a specified event e.g. sales campaign | • Demonstrates inter dependence of functions<br><br>• Provides overview of organization | • Some resistance felt to playing 'games'<br><br>• Not run in 'real' time so unrealistic | Senior management<br><br>Process training<br><br>Sales and marketing<br><br>Team building | Medium/High | Varies |
| **INCIDENT PROCESS (Critical Incident Method)** | The incident method is a variation on the case study but which seeks to provide greater realism by setting out the basic facts of an incident and then leaving the group to decide what further questions they need answered or information they require. | • Closer simulation of real life<br><br>• Permits sensitive or complex problems to be explored without risk | • Still element of artificiality | Problem diagnosis<br><br>Factual analysis<br><br>Managerial skills<br><br>Industrial relations | High | 10 maximum |
| **'IN' TRAY ('In' Basket)** | Exercise re-creating the working environment by providing sample letters, memos etc. from typical office 'In' Tray for group to evaluate. (See 'Training Methods' for more details) | • Immediately applicable knowledge<br><br>• Gives insight into work and standards | • Must be realistic | Time management<br><br>Stress control<br><br>Clerical skills<br><br>Supervisory skills | High | Small syndicates |

**Table 5.2** (*continued*)

|  | Description | Advantages | Disadvantages | Applications | Participation level | Group size |
|---|---|---|---|---|---|---|
| **LECTURE** | Verbal presentation of a single topic<br><br>Increase participation by providing opportunities for feedback (See 'Training Methods' for more details) | • High level of control over time and content<br><br>• Suitable for large groups | • Lacks interaction<br><br>• Low retention | Wide subject choice | Low | Unlimited |
| **PROGRAMMED INSTRUCTION** | Means of presenting factual information in a systematic way, generally by book or computer, so that after each segment (or 'frame') of information the trainee is required to test his understanding. If this response is correct the trainee will continue. If incorrect the programme will either indicate the right response or repeat the information again before checking understanding | • Learning pace set by indivdual/group<br><br>• Instant feedback | • Complicated to develop<br><br>• Required validation | General topics<br><br>New product information<br><br>Safety requirements<br><br>By-laws | High | Unlimited |
| **ROLE PLAYING** | Enactment of selected work situations allowing the group to explore variety of approaches to a given set of circumstances (See 'Training Methods' for more details) | • Enjoyable<br><br>• Develops empathy | • Can become frivolous<br><br>• Gauge of performance not problems | Interpersonal skills<br><br>Counselling<br><br>Human resource training | High | 6–8 |
| **SEMINAR** | Means of exploring specific topic by researching aspects in advance and exchanging information through reports and discussion with other knowledgeable group members | • Emphasizes individual research<br><br>• Encourages different perspectives | • Sucess dependent on knowledge of participants | Primarily used for conceptual or theoretical input | Medium | 10–20 |

**Table 5.2** (*continued*)

| | Description | Advantages | Disadvantages | Applications | Participation level | Group size |
|---|---|---|---|---|---|---|
| **SENSITIVITY TRAINING ('T' GROUPS OR GROUP DYNAMICS)** | Means of gaining insight into the effect of behaviour on others by encouraging members of the group to examine and comment upon both the behaviour of the group and the individuals who go to make up the group | • Widens understanding of human behaviour and responses<br><br>• Increases personal development | • Open and intensive nature can be intimidating<br><br>• Needs special training to handle high risks involved | Inter personal skills<br><br>Counselling<br><br>Communication | High | 8 max. |
| **TALK** | Less formal verbal presentation than lecture. Greater emphasis placed on exchange of information and opportunities for the group to respond | • Increased involvement<br><br>• Relaxed approach | • If group unresponsive becomes a lecture<br><br>• Possibility of losing direction | Most subjects | Medium | 10–20 |
| **TRIPS** | Group obtains direct experience of specific environment by visiting site and seeking answers to own questions | • Reinforces information given<br><br>• Gives sensory insight where words insufficient | • Can be perceived as a day out and frivolous<br><br>• Can require considerable organization | Operational training<br><br>Processes or mechanical courses<br><br>Supervisory or management programmes | Medium | 20 approx. |
| **WORKSHOPS** | Opportunity to discuss or discover practical approaches to handling given situation. Emphasis on practical realities rather than theoretical input and very job specific | • Transferable training immediately applicable<br><br>• Informality | • Different learning requirements of participants | Writing and communication skills<br><br>Complaint handling<br><br>Supervisory skills | Medium/High | 20 max. |

**Table 5.2** (*continued*)

| Read down columns Key: 1 = High 8 = Low | Knowledge Acquisition | Attitude Change | Problem-solving | Inter personal Skills | Participants' Acceptance | Knowledge Retention |
|---|---|---|---|---|---|---|
| Case Study | 4 | 5 | 1 | 5 | 1 | 4 |
| Workshop | 1 | 3 | 4 | 4 | 5 | 2 |
| Lecture | 8 | 7 | 7 | 8 | 7 | 3 |
| Games | 5 | 4 | 2 | 3 | 2 | 7 |
| Films | 6 | 6 | 8 | 6 | 4 | 5 |
| Programmed Instruction | 3 | 8 | 6 | 7 | 8 | 1 |
| Role Playing | 2 | 2 | 3 | 1 | 3 | 6 |
| Sensitivity Group | 7 | 1 | 5 | 2 | 6 | 8 |

**Table 5.3** Evaluation of effectiveness of training methods[1]

[1] From 'Evaluating the Effectiveness of Training Methods' by John Newstrom in *Personal Administration*, January 1980 (American Society for Personal Administration).

# Part 2  Delivery and Instruction Skills

# 6 Questions and Responses

---

▷          **SUMMARY**          ◁

- The ability to ask and respond to questions: an essential skill.
- Question handling and question formation, from both the trainer's and trainee's perspective.

---

## Asking Questions

In practice, there are two principal categories of questions.

1. Teaching Questions – which are designed to *develop* understanding.
2. Testing Questions – which are designed to control the group or *evaluate* the group's understanding.

Both of these play an important role in training and each one has particular properties of its own.

Teaching questions, for example:

- Arouse interest: asking a well-timed and relevant question can provide a change in the pace and direction and stimulate the group.
- Enhance participation: successful training depends on getting people 'involved'.
- Encourages thinking: even where the question asked is rhetorical and no response is required from the group, the effect will

still be to get the group thinking about the answer they might have given.

An illustration might be: 'Who hasn't, at some time, experienced a similar problem to this?'

Testing questions are useful to:

– Check understanding: although the most obvious reason for asking questions is to get answers, in reality the trainer is seeking to ascertain the group's understanding of the subject. Are there areas which need to be clarified, repeated or emphasized?

– Guide the group: if the group doesn't understand, further questions can explore the areas where help is needed. Similarly, where discussion has wandered away from the original topic, a well-structured question can return the group to the matter in hand.

## Types of Question

The principal types of question are:

| | | |
|---|---|---|
| open | leading | reflective |
| closed | loaded | focused |

### Open Questions

Open questions are ideal for encouraging two-way communication. They invite the person to respond freely and usually begin with 'what' or 'how'. An example would be: 'What do you regard as good service?'

### Closed Questions

The closed question is one which requires only a one word reply, often 'yes' or 'no'. Closed questions are useful for checking understanding or narrowing down options. Examples would be: 'Is this method right or wrong?' 'How many times did this occur?'

---

### TRAINER'S TIP

Avoid too many closed questions; they will inhibit participation and sound like interrogation.

---

### Leading Questions

The leading question, as its title suggests, is a question which indicates the response that the questioner wants or expects to hear. As an approach it should be discouraged because it prevents the person questioned from answering as freely as he or she would wish. It is often disliked as being a manipulative approach and can result in the questioner getting defensive.

Examples of leading questions are: 'You understand why we do it this way, don't you?' 'This would be a useful course for you, wouldn't it?' 'Wouldn't you agree that training would help?'

## Loaded Questions

Although both leading and loaded questions prevent the respondent from answering freely, the loaded questions is more subtle in its approach. The loaded question is biased to bring unfair pressure to bear on the respondent to answer in a particular manner. Examples include: 'Do you agree with the experts that Y is better than X?' 'You'd have to be mad to want Z wouldn't you?'

## Reflective Questions

Reflective questions can, at times, look like leading questions but they are used to reflect understanding, demonstrate comprehension to develop an answer or to encourage further discussion. Examples would be: 'So is what you are saying that without overtime these targets cannot be met?' 'Is your plan then to invest in new equipment?'

## Focused Questions

Focused questions provide a means of guiding the group by drawing their attention to a particular area. It is a particularly useful method of highlighting the learning points before looking at other aspects.

Examples include: 'So how many processes have we covered in this preliminary stage?' 'Can you tell us a little more about how you researched your market?'

# Asking the Right Questions

*What* you ask depends on *when* you ask it. You use questions at different points for different purposes.

In the beginning the trainer will use questions to establish the extent of trainees' existing knowledge. Once this has been established, it is possible to tailor the level and approach to suit the group.

During the course itself, questions are used to provide a change of pace, greater participation and to check that the information given has been satisfactorily understood. If further clarity is required, this will become apparent at this stage and areas of weakness can then be eliminated.

Finally at the end of the session, questioning is used to reinforce learning points and to gauge whether the course objectives have been achieved.

## Approach to Questioning

The approach most widely applied in posing questions is Socratic Direction. Socratic Direction in its simplest form starts by knowing the answers you want to receive and working backwards to the questions necessary to prompt these answers.

---

### TRAINER'S TIP

The stages of Socratic Direction can be easily remembered through the mnemonic KOPSA

K  *K*now the answers you want the group to provide.

O  *O*pen questioning should be used to tease out the answers.

P  *P*araphrase the answer once it has been given.

S  *S*ummarize all the contributions provided and stress these where it seems appropriate.

A  *A*dd any other information or explanations which will clarify the answer given before asking further questions.

---

It is important to emphasize that the ultimate purpose in posing questions is to receive an answer and lead to a wider understanding by the group. The objective is not to impress the group with the extent of your knowledge, nor to highlight the lack of knowledge on their part.

Questions should be framed in a way that won't embarrass or threaten an individual.

There are a variety of ways of asking questions but the three most often encountered are:

### Creeping Poison

This is where the questions are asked in sequence around the group so that group members can predict that the third question you will ask will be addressed to them. As a general rule this is an inadvisable method because it leads to increased pressure within the group. Group members can become so preoccupied about the question that they may be asked that concentration becomes difficult as they await their turn under the spotlight. Additionally, those who have already answered a question feel that they need not pay attention because the danger of being asked an additional question has receded.

The advantage of sequential answers is that it will ensure that everyone has an equal opportunity to answer questions and that no one person is overlooked or victimized.

## Heart Failure

(Sometimes referred to as '3P' questioning which stands for 'pose, pause and pounce'.) Heart failure is the exact opposite of 'creeping poison'. This is where a trainer questions individuals in the group without any prior warning. The random nature of the questioning technique means that the group has to 'keep on its toes' and pay attention, but the disadvantage is that the pressure of being put on the spot might result in blind panic, the mind going blank, or an ill-considered or garbled answer.

The Heart Failure approach is useful in focusing the group's attention and maintaining control.

## Popcorn Questioning

Popcorn questioning is less direct and so a less threatening method of questioning. In this approach the trainer poses a question to the whole group and, as with popping corn, allows the group to heat up gradually, answering questions as soon as they feel confident to do so. By providing the right environment and encouraging a response, soon answers should be 'popping up throughout the group'.

Popcorn questioning is useful where the individual group member could feel inhibited or where the intention is to enhance team spirit and gain greater participation. The approach is less formal but care must be taken to avoid the same people answering questions each time.

# Responding to Answers

The ability to frame a question in the right way is only part of the skill in questioning a group. The other major factor is in responding to the answers that the group gives.

When an individual answers a question, it is important to realize that the group will be looking at how that answer is received and how they would feel if they were in the respondant's shoes. Insensitively handling these responses can result in discouraging the group from any further participation.

## Reacting to Answers

### Acknowledge every contribution
Every response deserves some acknowledgement or comment. Ignoring a contribution is an indication that the response was unworthy of comment and will discourage that person and the rest of the group.

### Always acknowledge answers immediately
Whether the response is correct or incorrect, always indicate immediately. Failure to do so could result in learning points being missed or incorrect responses being assumed to be correct.

### Correct responses
Where the response provided is what was required, commend the responder, repeat the answer given and emphasize or expand upon the issue, moving on to further questions if appropriate. 'Thank you John. That's an excellent point. Financial considerations are not the only factor, human factors must also be taken into account. Can anyone think . . . ?'

### Broadly correct responses
If the answer given is broadly correct, emphasize the elements and seek further information about the remainder. 'Yes, the cost element is one factor here but are there any others we need to consider?'

### Incorrect answers
Don't dismiss incorrect responses without due consideration. Try to find something in the answer given which could be of merit. A possible approach might be to acknowledge the answer given, explore the reasons for reaching that conclusion and/or empathize with the respondent. Then either (1) re-state the question to provide an opportunity to the individual to correct that answer or (2) put the answer given to the group for comment.

1. 'Vernon, I can understand why throwing complaining customers out might be one way of dealing with the problem but do you think it would provide the best approach to handling customer complaints?'
2. 'So, Vernon, your suggestion would be to throw complaining customers out to discourage further customer complaints. Does

the rest of the group agree that this would be the best approach to handling customer complaints?'

### Where the answer doesn't make sense

Many people understand the question asked but find it difficult to put their thoughts into words. If the problem seems to stem from the inability of the individual to articulate his or her thoughts, the solution might be to help to clarify the underlying meaning and check back. 'So, Alan, if I understand you correctly, you would want to see more team involvement, is that right?' The objective is to clarify or paraphrase the individuals ideas, not to ignore them and impose your own.

### Where the response is completely irrelevant

In some cases, the answers given seem to bear little resemblance to the question asked. Before you start to question the sanity of yourself or the group, check that the question was understood and, if not, re-state in a clearer form.

The cause might be that some trainees are answering a question that they think you *ought to* have asked or that they believe you will be asking. In other words, their thoughts have outraced the issues under discussion. A response to this would be to thank them for the contribution and indicate that the topic will be covered at a later stage or that it touches on matters outside the boundaries of the present topic. 'Thank you, Derek, but you are way ahead of me. That's a good point that we will be pursuing later. Could you make sure that I cover it when we look at that topic next week?' Or 'Unfortunately we haven't the time to cover all the issues that could have an impact on taxation, Susan, but I would be happy to discuss these with you or anyone else during the coffee break.'

# Responding to Questions

As well as being able to ask questions, effective training requires that you are able to answer questions too.

It is always a wise idea to establish at the outset when you intend to deal with any problems or questions and, providing the group is made aware of the approach you will be using, this is largely a matter of personal choice.

There are a number of reasons for asking a trainer questions. The most obvious reason is to seek an answer to a particular issue.

### Genuine request for information

If the question is a genuine request for information, answer it concisely

**101**

and check with the questioner that this provides an answer that meets their needs. If further clarification is required, this can either be dealt with instantly, or suggest that the matter could best be discussed during a suitable interval.

There are also a number of less obvious reasons for posing questions and these include:

### Testing credibility

The object of asking a testing question is not about understanding but to probe the knowledge and expertise of the trainer. Often the test questioner already has the answer but wants to see how you handle it. If this is the case your credibility as a trainer depends on your honesty. Trainers are not expected to be the font of all knowledge but it is often felt that if they admit that they don't know they will lose all credibility.

*This is not the case*. It is infinitely better to remain silent and be thought a fool than to open your mouth and prove it beyond a doubt. If you don't know – *don't bluff*. If you fake an answer and you are found out, it will cast doubt upon everything that you have said so far.

On the other hand, being confident enough to admit you don't know implies that you feel sure about the accuracy of everything else you have said.

Providing the questioner doesn't seek basic information that you should know, the best approach is to congratulate the questioner on raising an important issue, admit that an answer doesn't readily spring to mind and promise to provide a definitive response tomorrow/after the course or later on. (Then make sure you fulfil your promise). The rule here is 'if in doubt find out'.

## TRAINER'S TIP

Where the information sought is basic information that you should know there is no excuse for not knowing it. However, one approach which might prevent you snatching defeat from the jaws of victory, is to commend the questioner and pass the question back to the group for an answer.

'That's an interesting question, Nigel. What does the group feel Nigel should do in those circumstances?'

This 'ricochet' approach should not be over-used and the trainer should take steps to redress the lack of knowledge as soon as possible.

### Displaying knowledge

The purpose of the display question is to impress upon others how knowledgeable the questioner is. All he or she is looking for is confirmation of his intelligence in front of the group and providing his facts are correct, you can win him over by flattery. 'Now that's an interesting question . . . not many people are aware of the problem associated with water treatment, etc . . .' If the information is not accurate, considerable care must be taken to reinforce those areas which are right and tactfully correct those areas where the questioner might be misinformed.

### The side-tracking question

The objective of the side-tracking question is to move the group's attention into an area which holds greater interest for the questioner. The reasons for doing this might be deliberate or unintentional but in either case the trainer should resist the temptation to be led off the track. 'We will be looking at just that problem tomorrow morning, Rose, so it might be better to save that question for then'.

### Challenge questions

Sometimes referred to as the 'Gotcha question', it often takes the form of using information provided by the trainer earlier to contradict the views currently being stated.

Your response in this situation is very important. The rule here is never take the criticism or challenge personally even if (or particularly if) it is meant that way! An emotional response will not be a rational one.

The correct approach is to pause, admit that the point is an interesting one, and use the time gained to think carefully about your response. If you can't justify what you have said *don't* try to. Defending the indefensible will mean that far from winning the person over you will convince the rest of the group of the validity of his concern. Instead, admit your mistake and emphasize the correct solution.

Equally if there is a good reason for the inconsistency of your answers, don't use this as an opportunity to score points. If you belittle the questioner in front of the group, at best he will be alienated, at worst he or she will seek revenge later. Demonstrate that you are above such things and you will gain the respect of the whole group.

## Do's and Don'ts of Asking Questions

### Do make sure that the question is clear

It is impossible to answer anything correctly if you don't understand the question. Avoid jargon and technical language which might not be understood, and phrase the question in a way that will not be ambiguous.

### Keep it short

There is little point in asking a question which is so long-winded or confusing that the respondent has to ask for it to be repeated. Where a question is complicated, break it down into digestible chunks.

### Keep it fair

The party questioned should be able to answer the question from the knowledge gained on the course or from knowledge he could reasonably be expected to have already. It is unfair to ask the beginner on a book-keeping course how to do a bank reconciliation if that is what they are there to learn.

### Do distribute questions evenly

Tailor the question to suit the person questioned. Part of keeping it fair is making sure that individuals don't feel that they are being victimized and that questions are always addressed to them. Questions are occasionally used as a method of keeping particular group members alert and under control. Although this is an acceptable approach it shouldn't be carried out in a manner which leaves the person feeling 'picked upon'.

### Don't ask 50/50 questions

Ask questions which require an answer to be thought out and not just to be guessed at. Avoid questions like 'which would you press, the red button or the blue button?'

### Don't ask vague questions

Questions like 'What is the first thing you would expect to see in any office?' are too wide or indistinct to be of any value. Questions should be precise enough to indicate the knowledge required to answer correctly.

### Don't seek public confessions

It is unfair to expect a response to questions such as 'Has anyone ever been ill through stress?' Even the most sensitive issue can be raised by questioning in an appropriate way. 'What sort of illnesses can be attributed to stress?' 'What sort of effects can stress produce?' will often result in a wider and more enthusiastic response.

### Don't ask questions reminiscent of the classroom

Classroom questions are those questions which can be completed in one word, such as 'We call this a . . ..?' with a pause for the group to provide a response. Similarly answers should be the product of thought and not rote learning as with A is for armature, B is for ballcock, what is C for . . .?

### Don't answer the question yourself

Trainers are often so concerned that they won't get the answer they want (or worse yet, any answer at all) that they finish up answering the question themselves. Don't give up too easily. If the group does fail to react it might be that they don't understand what you are asking, so phrase the question in another way.

►        CHAPTER REVIEW        ◄

**Developing and responding to questions is an essential trainer's skill.**

*Asking questions*
**Two types of question:**
     1. Teaching questions – which *develop* understanding.
     2. Testing questions – which control the group or *evaluate* understanding.

*Six types of question:*
     1. Open questions – invite a free response.
     2. Closed questions – can receive a one word reply.
     3. Leading questions – indicate in the question the answer required.
     4. Loaded questions – provide pressure to reply in a particular way.
     5. Reflective questions – used to demonstrate understanding.
     6. Focused questions – highlight particular areas.

*Approach to questioning*
**K –** Know the answers required from the group.
**O –** Open questions are employed to prompt these answers.
**P –** Paraphrase the answer.
**S –** Summarize all contributions.
**A –** Add any further information.

*Three methods of asking questions*
     1. Creeping poison – asking the group questions in sequence.
     2. Heart failure – addressing questions to individuals without warning.
     3. Popcorn questioning – seeking answers by encouraging group participation.

*Make sure questions are clear:*
     – Keep them short.
     – Ensure they are fair and distributed evenly.
     – Discourage guessing.
     – Avoid vague questions.
     – Avoid questions requiring a public confession.
     – Eliminate classroom type questions.
     – DON'T ANSWER QUESTIONS YOURSELF.

*Responding to Answers*
     – Acknowledge every contribution.
     – Respond to answers immediately.
     – Congratulate right answers.
     – Correct any inaccuracies.
     – Find merit even in wrong responses.
     – Check understanding.

# 7 Handling Problem People

▷                        SUMMARY                        ◁

- Some of the more problematical character types, and their distinctive behaviour.
- Suggested responses to neutralize these.

It has often been remarked, and it is undoubtedly true, that training courses would run a great deal smoother if they didn't involve people. Unfortunately, it is equally true that there wouldn't be much point in running courses without them. The only solution to this dilemma is for a trainer to develop a capacity to deal with different people and personalities.

Fortunately it quickly becomes apparent that although the individuals in the group are unique, the behaviour that they often display is more limited. This means that it is possible to recognize broad character types in the composition of any group even though not *all* characters will be present all of the time.

## The Talking Terror

### Character

The talking terror talks incessantly. In his most irksome form he is a loud mouth who dominates the group and monopolizes any discussions. In his less irritating, but equally disruptive form, he is the constant chatterer who has always had something similar happen to him. Whatever manifestation the talking terror might appear in, the group will be looking to you to maintain control.

### Causes

Although the end results may vary somewhat, the cause of talking terror is invariably the consequence of insecurity. The talker often feels that he must prove himself before the trainer and/or group. Consequently, he may spend much of his time trying to demonstrate to the group the depth of his knowledge in order to convince them that he is deserving of their respect (this is the 'know it all' talker). Or he may be seeking approval by showing his enthusiasm for the topic under discussion (the 'eager beaver'). Or he may just want to be noticed by the group as someone worthy of attention and acceptance ( the 'chatter-box').

### Favourite Phrases

'I believe I'm right in saying . . .' 'What I always do . . .' 'I'

### Control

1. Look for an opportunity to intervene. This may be a pause for breath or a moment's hesitation. Thank or agree with the talker (few talkers will want to interrupt this vote of support) and then, having regained the group's attention press home your advantage by redirecting their concentration elsewhere. For example: 'Yes, Max, that would make sense. Does anyone else know of ways that we could achieve this?'
2. Check your understanding and then move on. For example: 'Just a moment Max – so what you are saying is X, Y, Z; has anyone else got a view on this?'
3. Speak to him during a convenient break and explain that you are pleased that he is participating but that you want to involve other members of the group in the discussion.
4. Channel his energies elsewhere. Ask him to record all the ideas generated by the group on to a flip chart or seek his assistance as a technical operator for equipment or as an observer for the purposes of an exercise.

## The Great Griper

### Character

Although a certain amount of constructive criticism is often encouraged on training courses, the problem with the 'Great Griper' is that he regards *every* discussion as an opportunity to air his grievances about the company, the people he works with, the conditions he works under . . . in fact it could be anything at all. If he is allowed the chance to raise his 'pet peeve' his negative approach can completely undermine the enthusiasm of the rest of the group.

### Causes

The Great Griper needs to convince himself that he is entitled to feel the way that he does and that others share his beliefs. It's not that he actually wants to change anything, because even if the cause of his indignation was eradicated overnight, he would still find something else to moan about. No, the important thing is that while he can point to something that is wrong he can have a justifiable reason for behaving in the way that he does. His attitude is 'why should I put myself out to do X when life/the company/rest of the world – does Z?'

### Favourite Phrases

'The trouble is . . .' 'Well that's all well and good' 'But . . .'.

### Control

The danger in dealing with a Great Griper is that you can allow yourself to be drawn into a discussion on his favourite topic rather than dealing with the matters you should be covering. Don't get ensnared.

1. Allow him his say *once*. Let him clear it off his chest and then move on. 'Fred, I can see that you feel strongly about this. Supposing we set aside three minutes now to discuss this and then let's agree to drop the matter until after the course.'

2. Turn the problem round and ask him what he would do about the problem and what action he would take. It could be that a simple solution does exist, in which case why hasn't he acted upon it? 'Fred, you've explained the problem to us. What would you want to see happen to resolve it?' Acknowledge the gripe without accepting its validity and then:

3. Take some form of positive action to lay it to rest. 'I can appreciate why this might upset you, Fred, so let's get together at lunchtime and see if we can draft a memo to the MD/Sales Director/Chief Executive and get this sorted out.'

## Doubting Thomas

### Character

The Doubting Thomas or Thomasina is a variant of the Great Griper. The main difference is that while the Great Griper often has only one or two areas of sensitivity the Doubting Thomas has developed an all encompassing cynicism. Once again, if this negative attitude is allowed to develop it can be contagious and cast doom and gloom over the whole group.

### Causes

Invariably the Doubting Thomas is someone with a number of years' seniority. If this is the case his attitude may be the product of seeing many such bright ideas tried and fail. It could well be that some of the ideas that were never given a chance were his and that this has made him less receptive to the ideas of others. Finally, it might be that the sceptic (young or old) might feel that he might not be able to master these new approaches, processes, or procedures and therefore regards them as a threat best eliminated by dismissing with disdain.

### Favourite Phrases

'That'll never work.' 'We've tried that before.'

### Control

Gain acceptance step by step. First by getting agreement that if an idea or process did work it would justify the time and effort spent learning it. If this is forthcoming, albeit reluctantly, step 2 is to suggest that the Doubting Thomas agrees to suspend his judgement until the course is over and the end result can be evaluated.

If the Doubting Thomas does not believe there is merit in the process ask him to be specific about why he believes this and then seek his acceptance that the only way of proving who is right and who is wrong is by giving the process a fair chance. Then go back to step 2.

## The Pot Plant

### Character

The Pot Plant is so called because, apart from sitting in the group and looking decorative, she seems to contribute very little to the group except a touch of additional colour.

### Causes

There are all sorts of reasons why a Pot Plant might remain silent or withdrawn from the group, and not all of them arise from her own personality. It may be that she believes that if she says anything she will make a fool of herself and so feels inhibited. There again, the problem might not be inhibition but motivation. The topic could be one that the Pot Plant has no interest in and regards as of little benefit. Alternatively it might be that she finds it difficult to articulate her thoughts and finds it more comfortable to just sit and listen.

*Favourite Phrase*

'Sorry.'

*Control*

The approach that you take will depend on the reasons you feel the Pot Plant has for her lack of participation. In all cases your response should be to find a suitable opening to get the Pot Plant involved.

If you assess her reluctance stems from insecurity, build up her confidence before the group by directing a question towards her which you know she will be able to answer.

Where the non-involvement is through lack of motivation it could be that the Pot Plant doesn't appreciate how the topic relates to her. Take time to demonstrate the subject's impact. (You might also consider whether a more stimulating training approach might help).

If the root cause for withdrawal is an inability to articulate ideas, this can be quickly remedied by phrasing questions in a way that draws a response without requiring a full explanation. For example:

'Anita, do you find that asking closed questions can be a helpful means of overcoming shyness?'

'Yes'.

For those whose preference is to listen rather than speak it is for the trainer to accept that there can still be involvement without overt or active participation.

## The Jolly Jester

*Character*

It may seem hard to believe that anyone could take exception to the Jolly Jester. He brings a smile to everyone's face and can always be counted upon to have a merry quip to meet every occasion. In fact it is this capacity to find humour in any situation which appears eventually to drive the remainder of the group insane.

In moderation his sense of humour can be a considerable asset. It helps to break down barriers, relax the group and build up a sense of camaraderie. However, when subjected to frequent or prolonged exposure the effects can be likened to eating too much chocolate. After the novelty has worn off all that remains is an after-taste and nausea. The group lives in constant fear of saying something which might give rise to innuendo, *double entendre* or provide the cue for a joke.

*Cause*

It is unlikely that a Jester will ever realise the anguish that he often

**111**

causes through insensitive remarks or inopportune humour. In fact if these factors were pointed out to him the chances are that he would be devastated. His driving aim is to be 'one of the lads' and accepted as part of the group.

### Favourite Phrases
'That reminds me . . . ' 'I knew this man once . . .'

### Control
The difficulty in controlling the Jolly Jester is in maintaining the delicate balance between fun and over-indulgence.

1. The means of keeping control is to adopt the view that prevention is better than cure. Once he has begun a witty story it becomes almost impossible to cut him off mid-flow. So the moment he appears to be laying the foundation for a joke or humorous tale explain that there will be ample opportunity during the breaks or lunch to regale the group with anecdotes but that training time is at a premium. 'Sorry, Martin, I know that we would all love to hear what happened when you went for an interview but unfortunately we haven't the time now. Perhaps you could buy us all a drink at the end of the session and tell us then.'

2. Alternatively, use peer pressure to discourage him from making unwarranted interruptions.

## The Conspirators

### Character
Unlike the preceding categories, conspirators cannot work alone. For conspirators to work successfully they need to join forces with one or more people. Despite the title, their actions are rarely sinister, but arise from the manner in which they can be seen absorbed in their own private discussion in total disregard of those around them.

### Causes
Often the purpose of the conversation is to clarify a point that one of the party is uncertain about. Where the behaviour occurs immediately following a break it is likely to be to conclude a conversation started earlier.

### Favourite Phrases
'Where are we?' (Said in half whisper.)

### Control
1. If the reason for the conspiratorial conversation appears to be to improve understanding it may be that you are not explaining the

material thoroughly or that there is some confusion. In either case you will need to ask those involved whether a problem exists.

2. When the discussion appears to be unrelated to the training there are four possible approaches:

— If the conversation seems to be coming to a close ignore it and carry on.

— Stop talking and look at the conversationalists so that they become conscious that they are distracting you. If this doesn't happen immediately, wait and often someone else on the course will interrupt on your behalf.

— Ask them if there is an issue they would want to explore with the rest of the group. In practice this is difficult to say without sounding like a school teacher. The better approach would be to acknowledge that they have matters they wish to pursue but that they will have the opportunity to do so in 30 minutes when they break.

— Using the name of one of the conspirators, pose a question to them as if oblivious of their current conversation. 'Chris — Are there any other ways we might . . .?'

▶ CHAPTER REVIEW ◀

| Character | Description | Response |
|---|---|---|
| Talking Terror | Constant talking | 1. Look for an opportunity to intervene, thank them for contributing and quickly re-direct group's attention<br>2. Check understanding and move on<br>3. Seek co-operation<br>4. Channel energies elsewhere |
| Great Griper | Negative | 1. Allow opinions to be voiced *once* and move on<br>2. Ask for solution<br>3. Put matter to rest |
| Doubting Thomas | Cynical | Gain commitment to change |
| Pot Plant | Non-contributor | Discover the cause and seek chances for involvement |
| Jolly Jester | Joking | 1. Limit opportunities<br>2. Use peer pressure to inhibit |
| Conspirators | Whispering | 1. Check reason and resolve misunderstandings<br>2. Discourage talking |

**Table 7.1** *Problem types and how to handle them*

# 8  Building Rapport

$\triangleright$           SUMMARY           $\triangleleft$

This chapter:
- Introduces the concept of rapport.
- Demonstrates methods of achieving rapport through positive reinforcement.

One of the essential ingredients for training success is the ability to develop rapport or understanding with those being trained. This simple notion is a good deal easier to talk about than it is to achieve. The reason is that although reference is made to 'group training' there is no such thing as 'group learning'.

It may be more convenient or economical to bring people together for training but even if you train as a group, *you learn individually*. For learning to take place each of the members of the group must feel that you have taken account of their individual circumstances and have tailored your approach accordingly. The capacity to talk to a *collection* of people and yet to make them feel that you are addressing them *individually*, is a skill which takes time to achieve.

There are some useful pointers which can be provided to help you to build rapport.

## The Personal Approach

No one likes to believe that they are a faceless cog in a machine or a statistic in a training report. An important part in gaining individual support arises from recognizing individual contributors. When you receive a response to a question mention the responder by *name*, and thank them for making a contribution. This increases self-worth, their stature within the group and encourages others to participate.

## Encouragement

Encouragement in training is imperative. Unless participants feel that they can experiment with new approaches without fear of failure, they will never learn anything.

It is unlikely that you will achieve a completely care-free training course but it *must* be totally risk-free. That is to say trainees should not feel that if they do get things wrong they will put expensive equipment at risk, or jeopardise the safety of others, or the job for themselves. None of these factors prevents tests being set, grades being given or certificates awarded on completion of various stages but they should be scrupulously avoided during the acquisition of skills or knowledge.

As far as possible the atmosphere should be conducive to learning and not hostile, overly competitive or intimidating. The approach should be to build-up confidence by reinforcing the aspects which indicate that trainees are learning. This is achieved by emphasizing what they are doing right rather than dwelling on what was incorrect. 'Well done, Bill, your gear changes are much smoother and your steering has improved considerably.' *NOT* 'I've told you before – don't change gears without pushing in the clutch and you're still veering from one side of the road to the other.'

## Involving People

Following on from offering encouragement is involving the trainees in the learning process. Reference has been made to the fact that people learn most from direct experience. Participation is also an excellent way of developing rapport both inter-group and between trainer and trainees.

The best method of gaining this involvement is to design opportunities for participation into the training programme and to indicate clearly throughout the course that the group's contribution is valued. In many cases the value that trainers attach to group participation is apparent not only from their words but also from their deeds. The group will take their lead from a number of positive or negative signals that they receive from the trainer (see Table 8.1).

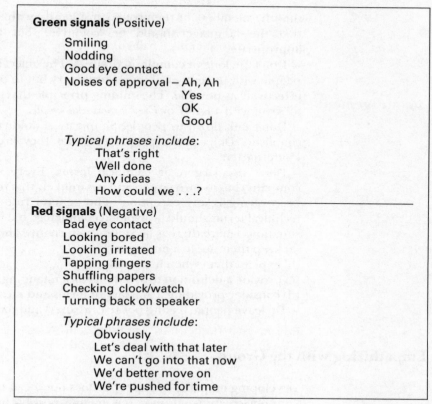

**Green signals** (Positive)

    Smiling
    Nodding
    Good eye contact
    Noises of approval – Ah, Ah
                     Yes
                     OK
                     Good

*Typical phrases include*:
    That's right
    Well done
    Any ideas
    How could we . . . ?

**Red signals** (Negative)

    Bad eye contact
    Looking bored
    Looking irritated
    Tapping fingers
    Shuffling papers
    Checking clock/watch
    Turning back on speaker

*Typical phrases include*:
    Obviously
    Let's deal with that later
    We can't go into that now
    We'd better move on
    We're pushed for time

**Table 8.1** *Signals from trainer to group*

## Providing Enthusiasm

Rapport is seldom obtained freely but, like respect, it has to be earned. The effort and enthusiasm that you put into delivering your subject will be more than compensated for by the interest and motivation it inspires in others as a result. Henry Ford maintained that enthusiasm is a prerequisite for progress in any field. 'With it there is accomplishment, without it there are only alibis.'

## Creating Understanding

For people to *respond* to what you say they must *understand* what you say. This means that the language you use must be of a nature and in a form that the members of the group can identify with. This doesn't mean that the language should be 'colourful' but that it should be appropriate.

– Don't use long or complicated words. The object is not to overwhelm people with the extent of your vocabulary but to convey a message as effectively as possible. The guiding principle that some trainers use is to 'say it with a KISS' or *Keep it short and simple.*

– Don't talk down to people. Simplicity shouldn't be confused with simplistic. Don't make people feel that they are in the corporate kindergarten.

– Don't use jargon or technical terms. Every subject (and every company) has its own jargon and it is unlikely that the area that you will be covering is any exception. The general rule is that jargon and technical terms should be avoided completely, but in those exceptional situations where there is no suitable alternative always:

(a) keep their use to a minimum;

(b) explain them when first used;

(c) provide a definition to avoid misunderstanding;

(d) consider providing a glossary of terms and meanings.

– Do leave people feeling positive, assured and motivated.

## Empathizing with the Group

Developing empathy with people does not mean that you should lose your objectivity as a trainer. It is not only possible but also essential that you appreciate any difficulties or problems that individuals may have *without* becoming involved yourself. (This detachment assumes even greater importance where the trainer's role includes counselling, observation or facilitation.) So, for example, you might show that you appreciate the obstacles that trainees might need to overcome in order to put their new-found training skills into operation without undermining the system itself. An illustration of this might be: 'I realize that when you are on piece work bringing the safety rail down can be time consuming, but putting your life and others at risk is totally unacceptable.'

## Highlighting the Areas in Common

It will greatly assist the development of a bond between trainer and group when the group appreciates that they share a number of aspects in common with the trainer. This means instead of the usual cursory introduction at the beginning of the course, emphasize any areas of your background that you might share or overlap with those of course participants and continue to do this whenever a common aspect appears.

## Aligning Yourself with the Group

The position of trainer lends itself too easily to the trap of setting yourself up as an expert. The moment you do this you distance yourself from the rest of the group. Similarly, avoid using phrases like 'you' or 'they' which indicate that you don't regard yourself as part of the group. The all encompassing 'we' can help to overcome this problem.

## TRAINER'S TIP

A technique used by the more astute trainers to establish rapport is to associate yourself with the group whenever there is a negative aspect, e.g. 'We have to develop better supervisory skills to succeed in business today', and to give complete credit to the group for any positive aspects, e.g. 'You've all shown that you can supervize effectively by reaching your current grades.'

► CHAPTER REVIEW ◄

**Although people may train as a group they learn individually.**

**Building rapport can be achieved by:**

| | |
|---|---|
| The personal approach | Creating understanding |
| Encouragement | Empathizing with the group |
| Involving people | Highlighting common ground |
| Providing enthusiasm | Aligning yourself with the group |

**Avoid:**

- Being patronizing
- Using technical terms and jargon
- Negative (red) signals

# 9     **Using Your Voice**

▷                SUMMARY                ◁

This chapter:
- Illustrates the role of projection, pace, pitch, pauses and emphasis in a good voice production.
- Describes some of the more common vocal blunders associated with training.

## Vital Vocals

Your voice is the means of carrying your message to the group, and used correctly it can be a powerful instrument. However, like any instrument, it needs practice and understanding to be effective. In the wrong hands (or throat) it can be an instrument of torture – monotonous and droning rather than a pleasure to the ear. Most people hearing their voices played back for the first time, are shocked and horrified with the result. Denial is a common emotion, followed by accusations of faulty equipment.

## Sound

The truth is that what *we* hear when we talk is very different from the sound received by others. This is because the jawbone acts as a diaphragm and the sound vibrates through the air passages connecting the mouth and ears. In such circumstances it would be little wonder if the voice wasn't distorted.

## Accents

No sooner has the initial shock of hearing yourself worn off than it is replaced by anxiety over your diction and accent. Unless your regional accent is so marked that what you say is completely unintelligible, then accept it as part of your personality. In fact take it one stage further and turn it into an attribute.

## Techniques

Whatever your voice may sound like there are still a number of techniques you can use to improve upon its effectiveness. The key factors in vocal success are:

Projection                     Pitch
Pace                           Pauses
and the odd one out: Emphasis

### Projection

If you have something worth saying you have something worth hearing. So your motto should be: 'Stand up, speak up and shut up.'

Use your voice to grab the group's attention. This doesn't mean that you should shout and bellow. Being aggressive isn't the same thing as being powerful. (It is possible to attract interest by speaking in little more than a whisper. If your voice is barely audible the group needs to listen carefully to hear what you have to say.)

Assessing the correct volume level isn't always easy. As the speaker you are closer to the sound source than everyone else in the room and this may give a misleading perception of volume.

The secret is to make full use of your innate ability to adjust volume to suit the circumstances. For example, when you are talking to someone standing directly opposite you, your mind will automatically gauge the level of volume necessary to carry your voice to them comfortably. Similarly if that person were standing on the opposite side of the road your mind would automatically compensate for the distance and traffic noise by raising the voice to a volume level thought necessary to reach them satisfactorily.

This same mechanism can be used in training by looking at the last row of trainees rather than those immediately at the front. The result will be that your voice will be projected to reflect this, and the sound will be carried, audibly to the whole room.

### Pace

The mind has the ability to process information far quicker than the mouth is capable of delivering it. The average human speech is about 150 words per minute. The net effect of this is that unless the information being communicated is particularly absorbing it is all too easy for the mind to use its excess capacity to think about other matters – the weekend, the weather, or lunch. If this mental jaunt is to be prevented then it is essential that the pace of the delivery is correct. If the pace is too slow or measured it creates the impression that the trainer is plotting his course as he speaks, which is hardly guaranteed to inspire confidence. (Should this ponderous approach be allowed to continue it will eventually send the group to sleep, which is even less inspiring for the trainer concerned.)

If on the other hand the delivery is too fast, the results can be very similar. Too much information, for too long, and the mind gives up attempting to process the barrage of data and just switches off. Getting the balance right means thinking about the information being communicated.

New or complex ideas should be delivered at a slow, steady pace with opportunities for the group to register the information and check their understanding. Where the information being communicated is background information, facts they should already know, or scene-setting details – these can be provided at a faster pace.

## TRAINER'S TIP

One of the dangers in slowing down is that there is a tendency to begin talking down at the same time. Don't let the delivery become patronizing.

Other factors which can influence the pace are:

– The more trainees there are the longer it will take to put your point across and register their response to it. This gives rise to the dictum 'more space less pace'. As numbers increase you will subconsciously slow down your delivery to check the response that your message is producing.

– Nerves. Tension increases the pressure to get the experience over as quickly as possible. The greater the tension, the greater the acceleration.

– Interest. The degree of interest that you share in the topic you are speaking on will slow you down or speed you up accordingly. The more enthusiastic you are the faster your delivery (although this will often be compensated for by talking for longer).

– Time. Where time isn't at a premium you can afford to meander through your material. In most cases, though, you will be racing against the clock and racing through your material.

If there isn't enough time to deliver all the information then cut it down. Structure your notes to allow non-essential or 'could know' (see Chapter 3) information to be circumvented easily. If you attempt to give all the information at twice the speed all you will succeed in doing is halving the understanding.

### Pitch

A common criticism of speakers is that they are 'monotonous' or one-toned. In reality it is impossible for anyone to communicate using a single tone and even the simplest conversation would use between ten and twenty different notes. What might cause this attitude to prevail, is that when training or speaking in formal situations certain speakers use a more limited scale of five to eight different notes.

The reasoning behind this seems to vary. It could be that by constant rehearsal and repetitions of the speech the trainer has lost the highs and lows which would occur quite naturally when the words were spontaneous. In some cases it is the deliberate style of speakers who feel that to add too much inflexion would make a serious topic too dramatic. Whatever the logic, the consequences can be dire. Varying the pitch of what is said helps to retain interest.

In some cases these pitch changes aren't intentional but occur because of stress. Tension in the body manifests itself by tensioning of the vocal cords. These shortened, and 'highly strung' vocal cords then cause the all too frequent strangulated voice or embarrassing vibrato effect. When you are tired the reverse happens and the cords lengthen and sag. The solution is to be conscious of what causes these pitch changes and what effect these can have on the group.

### Pauses

The power of the pause is generally underestimated by speakers. Some of the greatest speakers have learnt to master the art of silence, and comedians depend on it for their livelihood. The inclusion of a pause before a punchline is the essence of comic timing and serves a similar purpose in speaking to any group of people. Many trainers, though, feel very self-conscious using pauses because they believe that a pause might be seen as a sign of nervousness or indecision on their part. In most cases these fears are unfounded, providing that these pauses aren't unnecessarily elongated. Using a timely pause allows the group to assess the importance of what is being said as well as adding value in a number of useful ways:

- Before speaking.
  A pause allows time for you to gather your own thoughts and for the group to prepare themselves for the pearls of wisdom to come.
- As punctuation.
  Use a pause to paragraph speech or increase understanding: 'So there are two types of question we can ask (pause). These are (pause) teaching questions (pause) and training questions (pause).'
- Highlighting.
  Where a point is of vital significance but can be easily overlooked or misunderstood pausing, at the right moment, can amplify the meaning. For example, greater emphasis can be achieved by saying: 'You must . . . *not* (pause) on any account (pause) . . .' rather than 'You mustn't on any account . . .'
- After disruption.
  If a question has been asked or your flow has been interrupted, pausing after dealing with the issue signifies that the matter is now at a close and that you are returning to your original discussion.

### Emphasis

With any technique the key to success is to use it sparingly, and emphasis is no exception. There is little to be gained from emphasizing every other word in a speech, any more than you would wish to underline every other word that you write. The idea is to make the essential learning points or key messages as apparent and memorable as possible. Emphasis can be provided by:

1. Stressing certain areas: 'Training is about talking *to* people and not talking *at* them.'
2. Enumerating: 'There are three reasons for wearing safety goggles. One . . . Two . . . Three . . .'
3. Assertion: 'You cannot make omelettes without breaking eggs.' This approach requires the voice to be sustained to the end of the sentence.

# Common Vocal Blunders

### Fading

Faders are those whose sentences are so long that by the time they reach the end of them they barely have enough strength left to draw breath. The result is the last part of the sentence is as faint as they are.

Solution: Don't drop your voice at the end of sentences, and keep them short.

### Mumbling

Mumbling generally occurs when the trainer is unsure of what he is saying and therefore wishes as few people as possible to hear him. Solution: Either check on your facts or avoid doubtful areas.

### Gabbling

Gabbling occurs when a speaker either (1) omits words and/or syllables or (2) runs all the words together into one long sentence. In the race to return to a less exposed environment the presentation is completely incomprehensible, but it does have the advantage of cutting speaking time down by half. Solution: consciously slow the pace down and concentrate on your diction. True, this does prolong the agony by a few minutes, but that is a small sacrifice to pay for a better than average presentation.

### Mufflers

Muffling is another product of pressure and can be attributed to several factors. The most common cause of muffling for trainers is talking with your back to the group and addressing flip charts or overhead transparency images instead. Other forms of muffling include placing your hand in front of your mouth, speaking through clenched teeth or just speaking too softly. Solution: Assess your presentation style and take steps to eliminate any bad speaking habits by rehearsing your material.

► **CHAPTER REVIEW** ◄

**Concentrate on:**

| | | |
|---|---|---|
| Projection | Pitch | Emphasis |
| Pace | Pauses | |

**Avoid:**

| | |
|---|---|
| Fading | Gabbling |
| Mumbling | Muffling |

# 10 Non-Verbal Communication

▷            SUMMARY            ◁

This chapter:
- Emphasizes the importance of non-verbal communication.
- Highlights some of the movements and mannerisms associated with body language.

## The Importance of Non-verbal Communication

In earlier chapters it was explained that people learn best when they want to and when they believe that you, the trainer, have some knowledge that they would benefit by. This means that each member of the group must have confidence in what you have to say. The problem is that not everything that you have to say is actually said verbally. Although you *speak* with your *voice*, you *communicate* with your whole *body*.

If the group is to accept what you want to tell, them they must first have confidence in you as a trainer. It is an unfortunate fact that people judge the accuracy of the message according to the reliance they place on the messenger . . . You. This means that from the moment you first meet a group member, he or she will be assessing you to see how much validity they can place on what you have to say, how much authority you possess and the extent to which they can place their faith in you.

It is only once these points have been established to their satisfaction that they will relax and listen to the content of your message. This doesn't mean that the role of non-verbal signals ceases once this credibility has been established. It then plays a major part in creating group understanding.

The behaviouralist Albert Mehrabian discovered that as much as 55 per cent of a message's impact was construed from the non-verbal elements. Intonation contributed a further 38 per cent but only a paltry 7 per cent of understanding was distilled from the words themselves. It will be apparent from all this information that gestures, mannerisms and expressions can have considerable significance. In particular they:

1. Affect *receipt* of the message.
2. Affect the *understanding* of the message.

## Receipt of the Message

It is impossible for people to learn when they are nervous, and equally it is impossible for trainers to teach when they *communicate* nervousness. This doesn't mean that you must avoid training until such time as you can do so without a degree of stress, because an element of tension is essential and inevitable. What it does mean, though, is that the effective trainer must aim to look relaxed and in control *even* when the reality is a little different. If you don't look confident and comfortable, there is no reason why the group should be. Your manner should be:

friendly                      authoritative
approachable            confident

### Smile
The simplest and most effective way of demonstrating you are friendly and approachable is by smiling. This should be a natural relaxed smile not a nervous giggle, and certainly not a maniacal grin, which makes delegates wonder what you have in store for them. The less relaxed you feel the more important smiling becomes.

### Handshakes
Handshakes are a conventional means of breaking down barriers. They should not be seen as an opportunity of breaking down knuckles. Your handshake shouldn't be so flaccid that it is akin to shaking a wet fish nor so firm that it becomes a trial of strength.

### Posture
The way in which you stand can also provide a very clear indication of the way you are feeling. Your appearance should indicate that you are

in control. You must look authoritative without appearing militaristic. This means that if you are tall don't be self-conscious of your height and hunch yourself up like Quasimodo. Don't hop nervously from foot to foot or wobble about like a jelly on a plate.

### Demeanour

Your whole approach should be one of openness and assurance. Being self-assured isn't the same thing as being conceited. Nothing that you say or do should make the group feel inhibited, embarrassed or patronized.

### Appearance

It is often said that first impressions are lasting impressions and that you never get a second chance to create a first impression. This is unfortunately very true. When course participants attend a course they generally have formed some opinion of what they expect to see. Your appearance will form an integral part of this expectation.

If you would want the group to feel at ease and that you share the same values as they do, it is important to reflect the same dress conventions. For example, wearing an open-neck shirt and jeans when everyone else is wearing a suit may undermine your credibility and require you to work twice as hard in order to counteract this adverse initial reaction.

## Understanding the Message

The clarity of the message you are communicating and the conviction with which it is received by others, can be significantly affected by the non-verbal signals transmitted in the course of the presentation. Some of the factors which influence acceptance or non-acceptance are:

- Eyes.
- Arms and hands.
- Feet, legs and bodies.

### Eyes

The eyes are the most conspicuous channel of communication. In normal conversation the parties communicating would expect to maintain eye contact for 25 - 35 per cent of the time, and their eye blink rate would be approximately once every 3 - 10 seconds. During group training eye contact reduces dramatically and the blink rate increases.

Unfortunately, the manner in which our listening conventions have developed has been for eye contact and active listening to work in

**129**

unison. This means that we assume that if someone is looking at us when they are talking, then that information is intended for us. If on the other hand their eye contact is elsewhere we feel we can ignore the speaker and disregard what they are saying with impunity.

This can frequently be seen in group training sessions where a question is addressed to the group and eye contact is made with the group as a whole. The result is delayed response or no response at all. If the same question is asked while looking at an individual that person will feel compelled to answer or acknowledge it. The effect of this convention is that where there is insufficient eye contact with the group the rates of absorption and involvement also decrease.

If eye contact is so crucial why do so many people find it difficult? The answer undoubtedly is that because it is so powerful a gauge of our feelings we instinctively avoid eye contact in case others see how nervous or anxious we really are. In actuality this absence of eye contact confirms that the avoiding party is scared. Gaze behaviour of influential personalities shows that they make more frequent eye contact and hold this contact for a great deal longer than normal.

Far from interpreting the lack of eye contact as diffidence on the part of the trainer, it is seen by the group as demonstrating a lack of confidence, an intention to hide feelings or deceit. The solution is to

## TRAINER'S TIP

Establishing eye contact in circumstances which are nerve-racking or embarrassing can be difficult to achieve but there are two techniques which can be used to good effect to overcome most problems. These are:
  1. Lighthouse technique.
  2. Three step fixation.
1. Lighthouse technique
   This is where you use your eyes to 'sweep' over the group on a regular basis rather like a lighthouse beacon. If you feel that it would be disconcerting to make direct eye contact with members of the group, focus your sight on the area of forehead directly above the eyebrows instead.
2. Three step fixation
   As an alternative select three separate points around the room and at a level immediately above the heads of the group. This allows you to appear to cast your eyes about the group without the distraction of actually establishing eye contact.

make a conscious effort to look at people in the group – or at least to make them believe that you are.

## Arms and Hands

Possibly the greatest difficulty the trainer encounters when presenting material is what to do with his or her hands. In normal conversation your hands might not merit a second thought but somehow in making a presentation your hands suddenly seem to acquire the capacity to move independently of the rest of your mind or body. They can be seen tying themselves into knots, ferreting about in pockets and discovering nasal orifices they wouldn't dream of exploring generally in polite company.

What is it that causes this transformation? The answer is – nerves. Nervous tension results in excess energy to the system which needs to find a satisfactory outlet. In the absence of any obvious opportunity to work this energy off the body uses the only alternative available, which is to seek out something to toy with.

### Hands movements to avoid

#### Grooming
There is nothing intrinsically wrong in ensuring your tie is straight or your hair is in place. However, continuous patting and primping becomes irritating.

#### Fiddling
As a rule this involves small objects such as buttons, watches and rings, though other forms include toying with marker pens, paper clips and elastic bands. If you are conscious of being a 'fiddler' reduce temptation by keeping jewellery (pendants, necklaces, badges, cuff-links) to a minimum. Equally, you should keep well away from objects which are easily manipulated, such as loose change in trouser pockets.

#### Stroking
Akin to fiddling is comfort stroking. This invariably takes the form of stroking ear lobes or your neck, though more advanced forms include folding your arms across your body and hugging yourself.

#### Wringing
Hand wringing is a common occurrence and appears to an audience as a plea for clemency (which it often is).

#### Scratching
Of all the hand gestures, it is scratching which produces the most powerful response from an audience. The cause of this scratching seems to stem from a tingling sensation in the nerve endings brought

about by a change in the body's chemistry. The effect is to set the speaker into frenzied scratching which is soon mirrored by the rest of the room.

### When to use hand movements

Hand gestures should only be used to provide greater understanding to a group. They should have a purpose, they should be natural and they should be deliberate. Many speakers believe that if they make vague hand movements these will be less obtrusive and therefore more acceptable. These small jerky movements only serve to heighten your self-consciousness. If you want to move your arms do so intentionally, expansively and obviously. The main purposes for using hand movements are:

### Reinforcement

Hand gestures are at their best when they are used to reinforce what has been said verbally. In fact it seems to be impossible to ask for directions without receiving a verbal description together with a demonstration of winding roads and undulating hills reinforced by hand movements.

This process of supporting what is said verbally by using hand movements adds a further dimension to any presentation and can be viewed as an alternative form of visual aid.

### Emphasis

Emphasizing hand gestures differ from reinforcement gestures in that they do not attempt to describe a situation but rather to stress its importance. Pointing a finger, table thumping and karate chopping the air are all examples of emphasizing hand movements. Providing these movements are not over-used they can help communicate to the group the important issues.

## Feet, Legs and Bodies

Your standing *with* the group and their attitude towards you can be strongly influenced by the way that you physically stand *before* the group.

It is very difficult to convey an impression of controlled confidence when you are standing cross-legged and wobbling from side-to-side. The most authoritative posture is still regarded as standing upright. Not only does this provide good eye-contact and a command over the room but it doesn't constrict the diaphragm in the way that sitting can. An acceptable compromise would be to sit on the edge of a solid table. This has the effect of making the atmosphere less formal without inhibiting vocal projection.

Where an upright stance is used care should be taken to make it look relaxed and comfortable. Trainers shouldn't look like wooden soldiers nor stand like a reluctant nudist with their hands clasped in front of their body.

Moving about can, in certain circumstances, stimulate and refocus the group's attention. Equally, movement can become the source of considerable distraction and annoyance. Examples of those more common distractions include:

- Rocking forwards and backwards.
- Swaying.
- Emphasizing points by rising up on tiptoe.
- Performing a square dance.
- Standing on the sides of your shoes.

For movement to be acceptable it must be natural. Don't pace, pounce, wobble or sway.

► CHAPTER REVIEW ◄

55 per cent of a message's meaning is derived from body language.

38 per cent is delivered through intonation.

7 per cent comes from words alone.

Body language affects:

1. Receipt of the message.

2. Understanding the message.

Factors affecting receptivity:

| | | |
|---|---|---|
| Smile | Posture | Appearance |
| Handshake | Demeanour | |

Factors affecting understanding:

— Eyes – use lighthouse technique or 3 step fixation

— Arms and hands – avoid:

| | | |
|---|---|---|
| Grooming | Stroking | Scratching |
| Fiddling | Wringing | |

Use for – Reinforcement

– Emphasis

— Feet, legs and body – avoid:

| | | |
|---|---|---|
| Rocking | Swaying | Dancing |

# *11* Coping with Stress

▷                      SUMMARY                      ◁

- Guidelines for coping with stress.
- Some of the causes of stress.
- How to overcome common stress problems.

One of the most difficult aspects of the trainer's role and one of the hardest to equip trainers to deal with, is coping with the tension that has become an inevitable part of the job.

You are likely to suffer from stress whether you are a novice running his first training course or an accomplished trainer with years of experience. Too much work, too little time and last-minute programme changes play a part every bit as significant in the seasoned trainer's environment as they do in the world of the inexperienced trainer. If there is a difference it is that over the years experienced trainers have developed techniques to cope with this pressure and learnt to turn any nervous energy into a positive force. Many of these tried and tested methods are set out in the pages that follow.

## Coping with Stress

### Everyone Suffers from Stress

The first universal principle that needs to be acknowledged is that everyone irrespective of age, job or experience suffers from stress. Not only does everyone at some time or another suffer from nerves but research indicates that it is essential that they do so. A reasonable level of tension will set the adrenalin pumping and prepare the mind and body for the challenge ahead. The emphasis, though, should be on *reasonable*. Too much tension and panic will set in.

## Understand What Causes Stress

Once it has been appreciated that stress cannot be eliminated completely, the next step is to understand what causes this stress and how it can be reduced to an acceptable level. Our stress response is activated when we *anticipate* some form of threat that we *might not* be able to deal with (for example speaking to a reluctant group of trainees). This leads to a number of further steps.

## Stress is Subjective

If the stress response arises from *anticipating* some form of threat then it follows that if you assess the situation and believe that it can be controlled then (a) you won't feel threatened and (b) you won't feel stressed. On the other hand another person in exactly the same situation may interpret the situation differently and will suffer a great deal more stress as a result.

Stress is a matter of personal perception. What one person views as a potential problem another may regard as an invigorating challenge. Where one person looks forward to a social function as an opportunity to meet new people another person will see the gathering as a sea of hostile faces.

## Stress is Psychological *and Physical*

Having said that stress is a matter of personal perception, you might be forgiven for believing that this means that it is all in the mind. In reality the interpretive process might be attitudinal but the consequences are physiological and very real. When a stress response is triggered, the body physically prepares for the perceived threat by:

- Releasing adrenalin into the system.
- Increasing the heart beat.
- Altering breathing to become rapid and shallow.
- Dilating the pupils of the eyes.
- Tensing up muscles.
- Releasing sugar from the liver.

All of these are physical responses and all of them happen without any conscious desire on our part. A trainer taking his or her first course doesn't have to will the body to release more sugar from the liver. This will happen automatically and will happen whether he or she wants it to or not.

### Stress is 'Future' not Present

What very few people appreciate when thinking about stress is that it is all about the future. It is all 'what if . . .' Stress is a constant fear about what *might* happen. In reality our fears are often unjustified or unnecessary because, when the situation does arise we have little opportunity to think about how we feel. We just respond as quickly as possible.

## Stress and the Trainer

If our stress response is triggered by thinking about potential problems and anxieties over our ability to cope with them, what sort of problems might be faced by a trainer and how could these be overcome?

The answer would seem to be that most trainers are less concerned over the course content than over their own ability to stand up before the group and deliver the material in a coherent and effective manner. If this is the case, trainers are not alone. When 3,000 Americans were asked to rank their ten worst fears, speaking in 'public' was regarded as more frightening than financial ruin, spiders and snakes, and even death itself. This seem curious when death is a great deal more final than speaking badly in public. Set out below are some of the most common fears together with suggested methods of eliminating or reducing them.

## Drying Up

*Fear*
Drying up or 'corpsing' is a universal anxiety.

*Effect*
The effect is for the mind to go blank and to lose the thread of what is being discussed.

In practice the effect of drying up is seldom as obvious to the group as it is to the trainer. The effect of adrenalin on the biological clock is to speed everything up. This results in the trainer's perception that every pause or gap has lasted twenty minutes rather than a matter of seconds.

*Solutions*
– Keep clear notes with you as a safety net.

137

- Keep calm.
- Stop, pause, look at notes, *or*
- Repeat your last sentence (as if adding further emphasis) while you find your place, *or*
- Ask the group questions, e.g., 'Is that all clear so far?' 'Can someone give me an example of this?'

## Lack of Credibility

*Fear*
Belief that everyone will know more than you. Someone will ask awkward questions or the group will see through you.

*Effect*
Undermines the trainer's confidence and increases indecisiveness.

The best way of overcoming a credibility gap is ensuring there isn't one. That doesn't mean bluffing, but taking steps to redress any knowledge imbalance beforehand.

*Solutions*
- Find out about the level of course participants prior to the course.
- Read around the subject and not just a chapter ahead.
- Think about potential questions in advance. Certain questions will occur on every course.
- Speak to those who are experts before the course or enlist the assistance of those attending on the day. 'Joe, you've been using this new system; what problems have you found?'

## 'Uhmming' and 'Ahhing'

*Fear*
That unless some sound is made, there will be an obvious and embarrassing silence.

*Effect*
The result is the consequence of the mind searching for the next word and the mouth hoping to cover the silence by using meaningless sounds or expressions such as : O.K., Y'know, Right, Actually.

Even the most accomplished speaker 'uhmms' and 'ahhs' to some extent. What is important is that this doesn't reach the point where it becomes a distraction. Like nature, many trainers abhor a vacuum and feel the need to fill every silence.

*Solution*
- Know your material so that there is less need to fill in the silences.

   – Accept that pauses seem longer to you than to the group and don't
   feel embarrassed by them.
   – Breathe in silently instead of saying 'Uhmm'.

## Distractions

*Fear*
Concern that there will be someone in the group who will upset the
trainer's concentration. Most notable examples are where friends or
managers are in the training group.

*Effect*
Fear of looking foolish in front of the people you would most want to
impress. It is inevitable that sooner or later a friend, member of senior
management or someone you wish to impress will form part of a group
that you are training.

*Solution*
The solution is *not* to avoid contact with that person nor to address
everything to the individual and ignore the remainder of the group,
but to try and make things as normal as possible.
   Where the nature of the person involved is likely to make you feel
inhibited, visualize them sitting in the bath or wearing only a pair of
ankle socks. It becomes very difficult to remain in awe of authority once
these mental images have been created.

## Switching Off

*Fear*
Consternation that the group will be bored or won't respond.

*Effect*
Group will lose interest and become lethargic.
   Hard though it sometimes might be to believe, everyone in the group
will want you to succeed. No one comes along on a training course with
the prime objective of being bored senseless.

*Solutions*
   – Think about the group's needs in advance.
   – Have you included enough breaks or changes in pace and style?
   – Would visual aids provide greater clarification and stimulation?

– Could there be more opportunities to participate, feedback or interact?

## Fear of Making a Fool of Yourself

*Fear*
Consternation that the trainer will let himself and others down.

*Effect*
Making a fool of yourself encompasses everything from tripping over equipment to speaking nonsense.

Whatever the circumstances many of the greatest fears stem from fear of the unknown.

*Solutions*
It is difficult to suggest solutions to a problem which covers so many possibilities. Taking steps to discover as much information as possible builds confidence and eliminates the unknown element. Find out where the course is taking place, who is on it, what equipment is there and what the layout is.

## Missing Out Information

*Fear*
Concern over remembering a large quantity of material.

*Effect*
It is not unusual where a large amount of information is being delivered for material to be forgotten completely or to be remembered out of sequence.

The important point to emphasize here is that training isn't scripted like a Shakespearean play. Only you know what you intended to say and if you accidentally miss three pages or rearrange the material no one is going to ask what happened.

*Solution*
Where the subject is complex, break sessions into small units divided by interim summaries to reinforce learning and ensure nothing is overlooked.

## New Faces

*Fear*
Meeting up with a constant stream of new faces.

*Effect*
If meeting new people is a 'fear' rather than a mild anxiety, it is likely

that you will not feel comfortable running training courses.

That aside, many trainers feel a degree of trepidation before meeting people on a course.

*Solution*
Take time before the course to meet early arrivals, find out their names and background – and remember them. If it's appropriate, mingle over pre-course coffee and if it's not, at least direct them to the training room and help them to settle in. View the group as a collection of individuals rather than 'en masse'. Meeting and chatting before the course will prove to you that they aren't just faces and will establish rapport from the outset.

## Physical Effects of Stress

*Effect*
Shaking hands, knocking knees.

*Solution*
These are not as obvious externally as they seem to be internally. Don't try and control the shaking by holding on to equipment. Gripping a flip chart easel will only cause that to shake too. Diffuse the energy by natural movement such as pointing things out on the flip chart or giving out hand-outs.

Avoid small nervous or repeated gestures.

Use index cards for your notes – not paper, which rustles when you are nervous.

*Effect*
Palpitations. Caused by rapid heart beat and shallow breathing.

*Solution*
Slow yourself down beforehand by taking three deep breaths and holding each one for a count of three before exhaling.

*Effect*
Mild dizziness. Could be the result of moving too quickly or standing in one place too long.

*Solutions*
Sit down, or keep oxygen pumping round by curling and uncurling the toes within your shoes.

*Effect*
Dry mouth.

*Solution*
Where possible avoid drinking water (you are liable to gulp and get

hiccups). Avoid eating sweets or mints which you could choke on or swallow inadvertently.

*Gently* bite the edge of your tongue. This will produce more saliva and help to lubricate the mouth. This shouldn't be repeated too hard or too often or it will cause the tongue to swell and defeat the original purpose.

*Effect*
Wet mouth (Excess saliva). Caused by talking too fast and not providing sufficient opportunity to swallow.

*Solution*
Slow down rate of speech. Take a slow breath at the end of each sentence or topic. At a suitable moment pause, place your tongue behind your upper front teeth (as if to say 'T' or 'D') and suck in air with teeth clenched. This will dry the excess saliva without drying up the tongue. A dried up tongue will *stick* to the roof of your mouth.

▶ CHAPTER REVIEW ◀

**Guidelines for coping with stress:**

1. **Everyone suffers from stress.**
2. **Appreciating what causes stress can help to control it.**
3. **Stress is subjective.**
4. **Stress is both physical and physiological.**
5. **Stress is the consequence of anticipation.**

| *Problem* | *Solution* |
|---|---|
| **Drying up or corpsing** | – **Use notes** |
| | – **Stay calm** |
| | – **Pause and refer to notes** |
| | – **Repeat last sentence** |
| | – **Ask a question** |
| **Lack of credibility** | – **Check level of trainees' knowledge in advance** |
| | – **Read around the subject** |
| | – **Anticipate problems and questions** |
| | – **Speak to the experts** |
| **Uhmming and Ahhing** | – **Know your material** |
| | – **Accept the pauses** |
| | – **Use breathing as a substitute for uhmms** |
| **Distractions** | – **Visualize important people in ankle socks alone** |
| **Switching off** | – **Think about the group's needs in advance** |
| | – **Include breaks and changes in pace or style** |
| | – **Add visual stimulation** |
| | – **Provide interaction** |
| **Fear of appearing an idiot** | – **Build confidence** |
| | – **Eliminate foreseeable difficulties** |
| **Missing out information** | – **Divide up complex material** |
| | – **Incorporate interim summaries** |
| **New faces** | – **Meet group beforehand** |

*Physical effects of stress:*

| | |
|---|---|
| **Shaking hands and knocking knees** | – **Use natural movements to diffuse energy** |
| | – **Use index cards** |
| **Palpitations** | – **Use breathing to slow down** |
| **Dizziness** | – **Keep oxygen going to brain** |
| **Dry mouth** | – **Bite edge of tongue** |
| **Wet mouth** | – **Slow presentation down** |

# *12* Visual Support

▷                      SUMMARY                      ◁

- Why you should use visual support.
- When you should use it.
- What the choices of support are and the advantages and disadvantages of each.

You can often hear it said that 'a picture is worth a thousand words' and to a large extent this is undoubtedly true. What is missing is the inclusion of the word 'good'. Only a *good* picture is worth a thousand words. If the picture is blurred, inaccurate or irrelevant, the response is likely to be less enthusiastic.

The same can be said of visual support or visual aids. For visual equipment of any kind to be used effectively it is essential for the trainer to recognize that it is there as a *supplement* to him or her, not as a *substitute*. Visual aids are just that: visual media used to aid or enhance the trainer's presentation. Too many trainers relegate themselves to a walk on part instead of a starring role in their own presentation.

## Why Use Visual Support?

Visual aids are good servants but very bad masters. They should be regarded as a means of communicating your message more effectively and not as a magic wand to turn second-rate course content into first-rate training. Researchers estimate that the presence of *appropriate* visuals can result in up to 95 per cent of information being retained.

Visuals are over four times more powerful than words alone and nearly as powerful as experiencing situations first hand (which, for obvious reasons, have the greatest impact).

## When to Use Visual Support

There are five situations where visual support can make an effective contribution to any training.

1. Where the subject matter is complex.

In those situations where the topic is complicated, or deals with abstract issues such as ideas or concepts, using well-constructed visuals can help clarify the incomprehensible. It might be difficult to *explain* the Law of Gravity but a demonstration could make an impact in a way that words never would.

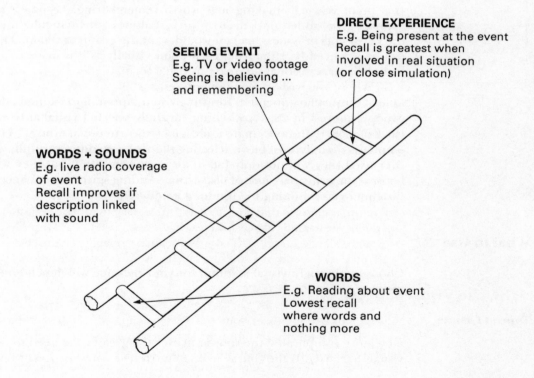

**DIRECT EXPERIENCE**
E.g. Being present at the event
Recall is greatest when
involved in real situation
(or close simulation)

**SEEING EVENT**
E.g. TV or video footage
Seeing is believing ...
and remembering

**WORDS + SOUNDS**
E.g. live radio coverage
of event
Recall improves if
description linked
with sound

**WORDS**
E.g. Reading about event
Lowest recall
where words and
nothing more

**Figure 12.1** *The learning ladder*

2.  Where there is a need to show relationships.

It is a great deal easier to show organizational links by using a visual format than to attempt to describe the same relationships verbally.

Similarly where there is a requirement to show how one process relates to another the simplest method is to use a visual medium such as a flow chart in preference to a lengthy description.

3. Where statistical information is involved.

Many people find figures and financial data difficult to grasp and even those who have a head for statistics will find that there comes a point where their mind cannot process the data involved. Visual presentation offers a solution to these problems by allowing one set of sales figures, for example, to be displayed alongside those for the previous quarter. This reduces the strain on the memory to a minimum and allows the group to concentrate on the learning points which can be distilled from the data.

4.  Where reinforcement should be given.

If a point is worth making it is worth remembering. Using visual support gives added impetus to your verbal message by highlighting the key points or issues that you would want the group to retain. This can be achieved by enhancing each point visually as it is made or by including an occasional summary in visual form.

5.  Where you wish to maintain interest.

One of the primary purposes for using visual support is to maintain the group's interest in the topic. Using carefully selected visual aids will extend concentration spans and increase understanding. The emphasis though must be on selecting the visual medium carefully. If over-used they will not only fail to assist concentration but they will become the principal cause of distraction. Adding spice may enhance a dish but over-seasoning will render it inedible.

## What to Use

Choosing the right visual medium for your message will depend on a number of factors.

### Type of Course

The more complicated the subject matter the greater the need to use visuals to clarify. If the course seeks to introduce a new process which has not been seen previously it might be easier to demonstrate this by using a model set up rather than relying on a verbal explanation alone.

**Group Size**

The medium chosen must be the most suitable for the numbers attending. A flip chart might be an effective method of communicating ideas to a group of eight but it is unlikely to be appreciated where thirty or forty are involved.

**Cost**

The group size and the subject matter might also have some influence in the financial resources available. If the course is going to be run regularly for a high number of participants and for a considerable period it makes good economic sense to invest in visual aids that are durable and easy to use. If, on the other hand, the course is only going to be run once and on a low budget, you will receive little thanks for incurring the cost of 35mm slides when overhead projector transparencies would be every bit as effective.

**Facilities Available**

It also makes good sense to use a visual medium which fits in with the equipment and facilities available. Computer graphics might seem like an excellent idea at the time but unless the hardware exists to relay the data on the course, it will be money and effort thrown away.

The opposite side of the coin is that all too frequently trainers decide that as they have the latest technology they will use all the equipment they have. In the same way that a chef who uses all his saucepans and kitchen equipment can clutter up his kitchen, so too a trainer who uses all the training resources can clutter up the training room and the minds of the trainees.

---

## TRAINER'S TIP

The best remembered messages are those delivered simply. Using the most up to date equipment doesn't guarantee instant success.

---

## Types of Media Equipment

This section will provide a brief insight into the presentation media starting with the most straightforward examples and progressing

147

through to the more complex formats. The applications of each method will be identified together with any inherent advantages or disadvantages.

## Flip Charts

Flip charts are simply large pads of white paper stapled together and punched with holes for displaying on an easel.

### Paper
Most flip charts are about 25" × 32" (635mms × 813mms) in size although smaller versions are available for desk-top easels.

Although there is a universal style, the quality and type of paper can vary considerably. Cheaper versions, not surprisingly, have cheaper paper quality which can cause the ink from one page to 'bleed' through to the page beneath, leaving arbitrary markings on the next sheet. This can be prevented by buying non-bleed pads or, where the chart is being prepared in advance of the course, inserting a spare sheet beneath the page being worked on.

It is a good idea to incorporate a blank page between different pages of the chart in any event. This prevents the group attempting to discern the next part of the chart through the current page.

Additionally, if you expect to carry out a number of calculations or to prepare bar charts or other graphics it is also possible to obtain flip charts printed with feint squares invisible from a distance but ideal as a guide for the trainer.

### Pens
Whenever you intend to use flip charts make sure that an adequate supply of suitable marker pens exists and that they *work*. Nothing is more infuriating than trying to write with a squeaking spirit marker whose spirit and ink has evaporated.

Test pens out in advance, replace the caps immediately after use and make full use of the range of colours available to you. In fact the safest way of ensuring everything works the way you would like is to carry your own supplies with you. These supplies should also include some 'blu tac' or masking tape to display completed charts around the room and two bulldog clips to attach the flip charts to the easel where the screws have gone missing (as they frequently do).

### Writing
Writing on flip charts is quite a skill. You need to think of what you want to write in advance and then visualize it magnified four times larger. The larger the group the larger the lettering needs to be.

As a general guide '8 by 8' is a good rule of thumb. In other words limit the number of words to eight per line and the number of lines to eight per page.

Make the lettering work for you, make it attention grabbing and memorable. Use visual puns to add impact (see Fig 12.2).

### TRAINER'S TIP

Make your visuals visible:
- Use block capitals in preference to lower case.
- Use colours to make it eye-catching.
- Leave spaces to ensure that it is legible.
- Use graphics to stimulate and make messages memorable.

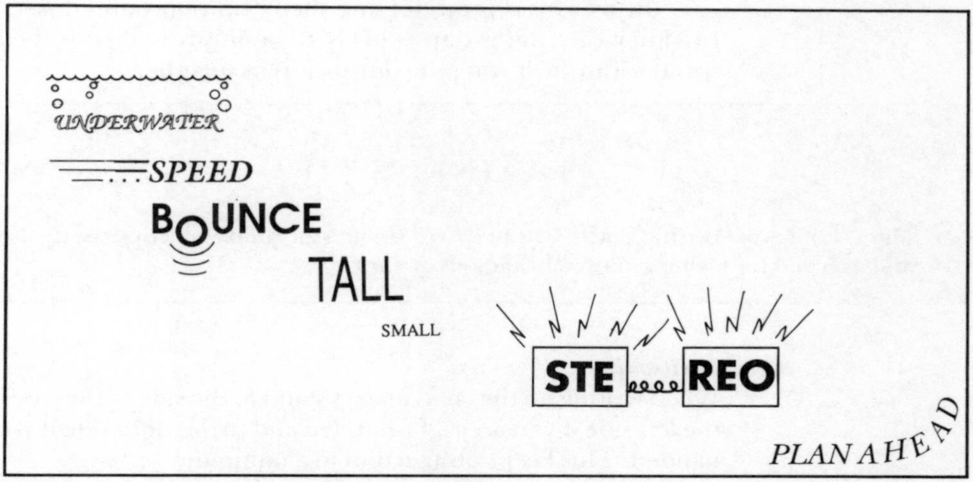

**Figure 12.2** *Lettering using visual puns*

Some trainers get anxious about writing on flip charts with a group looking on. They are concerned that their writing or spelling will let them down. If this is the case try the television cook's approach by preparing the finished product earlier. This saves red faces all round and allows you the time to write legibly and check your spelling beforehand.

Even in those situations where the flip chart is being used to record spontaneous contributions from the group during the course it is still possible, with a little bit of forethought, to predict what some of the responses will be. If it seems likely that one response to 'benefits of training' will be 'increased efficiency' head up a sheet of paper with the title 'Benefits' and write faintly in pencil on one side the correct spelling of 'efficiency'. This will allow you to write the response correctly if and when it is given by the group.

Pencilling information faintly on to the flip chart is invisible to the group and can be used to good effect in a variety of other ways too. If your artistic talents would make matchstick people look advanced, try drawing a faint outline of the picture beforehand. If you can't draw there are two other options available to you:

1. Enlist the assistance of someone else who *can* draw.
2. Try projecting the required image on to the blank flip chart using the overhead projector and then drawing round this.

In either case the group is likely to be impressed with the lightning speed with which you put your pictorials together.

## TRAINER'S TIP

Many trainers use two flip charts. One prepared prior to the course which can be used again and a second for taking group contributions on the course.

### Positioning

When writing on the chart always stand to the side of the easel. Stand to the left side if you are right-handed and to the right side if you are left-handed. This keeps obstruction to a minimum.

Obstruction can also be a problem when trainers speak and write at the same time. Although this appears to save time it means that the group will be reading what is being written rather than listening to what is being said. This is even more likely to happen when the voice is muffled by speaking to the flip chart and not to the group.

Always address the group and not the flip chart.

### Easels

Wherever possible use telescopic flip chart easels which can be adjusted to suit your height. It is difficult when you are a short trainer turning over the pages of a flip pad (and jumping up and down does little to assist credibility).

Avoid placing easels against sources of bright light such as windows because this can make them difficult to read.

Never hold on to the easel for support; it can let you and itself down without any warning.

### Advantages and disadvantages of flip charts

| Advantages | Disadvantages |
|---|---|
| Easy to use | Difficult to write on quickly |
| Economical | Only suitable for smallish groups (30 or less) |
| Instant visuals | |
| Versatile | Awkward to flip backwards and |
| Can be prepared in advance | Forwards |

*Applications*
- Use for recording group responses or feedback.
- Providing a regular summary.
- Making key points memorable.

## Whiteboards

Whiteboards carry on where blackboards left off. They are literally white boards with a gloss covering which permits multi-coloured dry marking pens to be used and wiped away.

### Advantages and disadvantages of whiteboards

| Advantages | Disadvantages |
|---|---|
| Easy to use | Special *dry* marker pens must be used or the material is non-erasable |
| Easy to correct | |
| Uses colour | Reminiscent of the school classroom |
| Economic once installed | Not portable |
| | The gloss surface reflects light and can make the contents difficult to read |
| | Once erased there is no permanent record |

151

*Applications*
- Spontaneous responses.
- Recording ideas.
- Clarifying technical issues.

## Overhead Projectors

The overhead projector (or 'OHP' as it is more commonly known), is one of the most versatile mediums for visual presentation. Unfortunately it is also the form most frequently mismanaged.

At its simplest it is a metallic box containing a lamp which projects the image from a transparency placed on top, through a series of lenses and mirrors to a screen beyond. As the lens has a fixed focal length, the image projected is controlled by the lens-to-screen distance. This means that it is necessary to experiment by moving the OHP backwards and forwards to establish the clearest image.

The overhead projector has become one of the most misused forms of visual aid equipment in a variety of ways. For one thing, contrary to its title, it is seldom used to project an image *overhead*. Generally it is used to project an image at eye level. This might prevent the group suffering neck ache but it also means that the view is obscured by the trainer or other members of the group. On those rare occasions when the view isn't obstructed by the audience, it will be obscured by the machine itself. The correct approach is to place the OHP down low and project the image up high.

### Keystoning

Another difficulty to overcome is the keystone or wedge shape which is caused by the OHP not being 90° to the screen. The result is that the image is distorted by being wider at the top than it is at the bottom. This can be overcome by either tilting the screen forward from the top or by raising up the front of the OHP. (Some modern projectors include adjustable front feet to allow this). If you choose to lift up the front of the projector you might need to use the locating pins or some form of chock to prevent the transparency from sliding off the platen.

### Transparencies

Considerable care should also be taken over the preparation and presentation of transparencies.

Transparencies (sometimes referred to as vu-foils or acetates) are only as good as their originals. So it is imperative that the best possible originals are used to generate transparencies and that these originals are kept separate for use on later courses if needed.

Although a number of companies do exist who professionally produce transparencies, the range of presentation materials and the availability of photocopiers makes it possible for anyone to create quick, economical and effective acetates.

As with all visual aids, transparencies should be bold, simple and easy to read. Any lettering must be large, and graphics should be colourful.

It is also advisable to put transparencies into cardboard frames or mounts. These prevent acetates from sticking together (a particularly prevalent practice when the trainer is nervous).

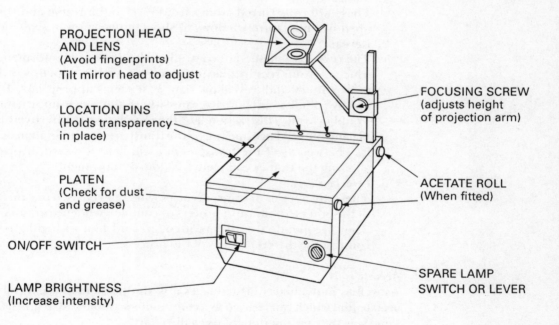

PROJECTION HEAD
AND LENS
(Avoid fingerprints)
Tilt mirror head to adjust

FOCUSING SCREW
(adjusts height
of projection arm)

LOCATION PINS
(Holds transparency
in place)

PLATEN
(Check for dust
and grease)

ACETATE ROLL
(When fitted)

ON/OFF SWITCH

LAMP BRIGHTNESS
(Increase intensity)

SPARE LAMP
SWITCH OR LEVER

**Figure 12.3** *Overhead projector*

## TRAINER'S TIP

By writing the learning points illustrated by each transparency on the cardboard surround of the frame it is possible to turn the frame into a useful lesson prompt for the trainer.

Each frame should also be labelled with a suitable title explaining the content of the transparency and allotted a number to allow easy retrieval and storage.

The disadvantage of using frames is that you can lose up to ¼" (or 6mm) of transparency the whole way round. Try to limit the image area of your transparency to a maximum 7.5 ins × 9 ins (191mm × 229mms).

Three additional techniques can add a professional touch to any acetates.

1. Masks.

    These are constructed from card, taped to the frame and then open like miniature windows to show information in sequence.

2. Reveal.

    The reveal is a method of controlling the amount of information which a group sees by placing a piece of card or paper over the transparency and 'revealing' data as it seems appropriate. It is ideally suited to lists or diagrams where too much information would provide a distraction. For the reveal to work effectively try placing the card or paper *under* the transparency rather than over it. The weight of the transparency will hold the card in place, allowing the trainer complete freedom of movement.

3. Overlays.

    These are a series of transparencies which can be used one on top of the other to build-up a process or complex sequence gradually. They frequently use different colour and film to highlight or contrast the different areas of the process.

### Acetate rolls

As well as individual transparencies it is also possible to use a roll of acetate film which can be used as a continuous scribble pad in much the same way that a trainer might use a flip chart.

### OHP techniques

For a piece of equipment that is no more than a light box with lenses it is surprising how easy it is for the unsophisticated overhead projector to outwit its human operator.

Here are some Do's and Don'ts which, when followed slavishly, can redress the balance.

*DO'S*

*Do* limit the number of transparencies shown.

There is always a tendency to provide too many rather than too few acetates. Each transparency you use will take time to set up correctly. It seems a shame when you have made the effort to produce visual support that they are then flashed on the screen and then off again before anyone has a chance to appreciate them. They may be familiar to you but this is the first time this group may have seen them. It will also take at least 15 seconds for the group to read and absorb the information displayed. If you use too many acetates all you will succeed in doing is subjecting the group to motion sickness and confusion.

*Do* get to know the equipment.

There are various models of overhead projector and although they often have the same capabilities their designs can differ dramatically. Take time beforehand to familiarize yourself with how this particular overhead projector operates and the layout of the switches. Is there a spare bulb and if so does it slide into place by a lever or on turning a knob? It's too late to muse about such things when the bulb blows in the middle of a training course.

*Do* set up the equipment beforehand.

This is linked with knowing the equipment. Get into the habit of running through some pre-course checks, including setting up and focusing the overhead projector. Use the first transparency you are going to show as the test acetate and leave it on the platen ready for its debut. There is no reason why the first few minutes of any OHP presentation should be spent trying to get the transparencies into focus. At the same time check that there is a clear view of the visuals from all the seats in the room.

*Do* remove visuals when they are no longer relevant.

The moment a transparency ceases to be relevant it starts to become a distraction. Don't be responsible for undermining your own training. If it's no longer relevant, be brutal, switch off and remove the transparency before the group switch off to you.

*Do* allow for further copies.

There must be some way of making replacement copies should the initial copy be lost or destroyed. Keep original artwork safe and separate. If you are likely to need to refer to an acetate at other points in the course avoid frantic searching for the only version by making additional copies. When you have shown a transparency remove it and place it face down in a separate pile.

*DON'TS*

*Don't* switch on without a transparency in place.

Get into the routine of always having a transparency in place when you switch on the OHP. The correct procedure is:

(i) line the acetate up on the platen, (ii) switch on the OHP, (iii) explain the reason for showing the transparency, (iv) switch off and then (v) remove the acetate.

This might seem a lengthy and unnecessary process but the alternative is a more amateurish and clumsy presentation. If you switch on without an acetate in place the blank screen will become the focus of the group's attention, as they look on with anticipation for what is to follow. While they are absorbed in looking they are not involved in listening.

Trying to align the transparency while the OHP is on will dazzle you, produce distracting shadows on the screen and give a preview to your transparency which results in lost impact.

*Don't* talk to the visuals.

There is a dual aspect to this requirement. First, don't talk while the visuals are *being displayed*. As mentioned earlier it takes a minimum of 15 seconds for a group to read a transparency. It will take considerably longer for them to consider its content and work out their response to it. This means you should give them that time uninterrupted. If you are talking in the background then what you say will be lost in the ether. You'll know when they are ready to listen because the eye contact will return to you.

Second, don't talk to the visuals *on the screen*. True, you have spent a great deal of effort composing your acetates but this is no reason why the group should have to make the choice between looking at the screen or the back of your head. The screen is *not* a prompt for the inadequately rehearsed trainer. If you know your material you will only need a cursory glance to check that the acetate is focused and centralized correctly before continuing. An alternative is to use prompts written on the transparency mount previously and read while aligning the acetate on the projector (see 'transparencies' earlier).

*Don't* get in the way of the image.

It can be very disconcerting, not to mention unprofessional, when a transparency is seen projected on the dazzled face of a trainer as he or she attempts to adjust the projector or point things out on the foil.

It shouldn't be necessary to continually alter the position of the OHP or fine-tune the focus for each transparency. Equally, it should be possible to point things out on the screen without standing on tip toe, stretched in front of the screen and blinking like a rabbit in a headlamp.

The essential aspects of the transparency can be highlighted by pointing them out on the transparency itself by using a pencil, pen or pointer. Where the trainer is concerned that his nervous shaking might be all too apparent if he holds the pointer, this can be overcome by placing the pointer flat on to the glass platen and then moving the pointer about as circumstances dictate.

### Advantages and disadvantages of the OHP

| Advantages | Disadvantages |
|---|---|
| Used in normal lighting conditions | Can be distracting or noisy |
| Straightforward operation | Prone to bulb/machine failure |
| Can be transportable | |
| Transparencies easily carried | Requires screen/matt white wall |
| Transparencies prepared in advance | Minimum projection distance on to |
| Economical | screen necessary to |
| Suitable for most size groups | avoid blurring (3-4 metres approximately) |

Applications
 – Pictorial or diagrammatic data displayed well.
 – Not suitable for large amounts of text.
 – Can be created in front of the group from group's own input.

## 35mm Slides

The use of 35mm slides in training presentations is becoming an increasingly common occurrence. Modern technology has meant that the noisy, cumbersome still projectors reminiscent of the classroom have become a thing of the past. Today's slide projectors are quiet, efficient and easy to use. Many of them have remote controls and most work on a cassette or carousel basis.

This increased popularity is reflected in the number of companies offering professional slide production facilities. This doesn't mean that slides can only be produced by professionals. Any reasonably competent photographer can make up slides using ordinary cameras and development facilities.

The same rules apply to the use of slide projectors as with most audio visual equipment. Make sure that you understand how they work.

Always follow the manufacturer's instructions and practise beforehand.

### 35mm slide techniques

There are, however, a number of techniques to using a slide projector effectively.

### DO'S

*Do* load the slides correctly.

Most carousel trays hold about 80 slides and loading these seems to cause the greatest obstacle to using projection visual support successfully. Each slide should be placed in the tray top first so that the slide is *upside down*. One of the most common mistakes is to believe that it is also necessary to turn the slide over. You *do not* have to turn slides back to front.

*Do* focus equipment in advance.

Once focused the projector should not need to be touched again. So focus the projector before the session begins. A useful addition to your equipment is a cloth suitable for ensuring the lens is dust and grease free. Many blurred images are the result of greasy finger marks on the lens. It is also worthwhile at the same time checking that the screen is clean and that the image can be seen without difficulty from all seating positions in the room.

*Do* make sure that slides are legible.

There is little point in making sure the projector is focused correctly if the slides cannot be read. Visual aids need to be visual. This means limit the text on each slide. Anything that is capable of being written down is capable of being spoken.

## TRAINER'S TIP

When words are necessary lettering must be a minimum of $\frac{1}{4}''$ (6mm) high to be seen.
A rough guide would be:

- Where the distance from screen is 12 metres (39 feet) or under the lettering should be 6mm high.
- Where the distance from screen is between 12 and 15 (49 feet) metres the lettering should be 12mm high.
- Where the distance from screen is between 15 and 20 metres (65 feet) the lettering should be 18mm ($\frac{3}{4}''$) high.

A quick check can be achieved by holding the slide at arm's distance and seeing how much of the information is clearly visible.

Careful consideration should also be given to the colours that are used on any slide. Reds and greens are usefully associated with stop and go/positive and negative – but they are also the colours which are most difficult to discern if you are colour blind. Some other colours such as blue on black just don't show up at all.

*Do* check the room can be darkened.

For slides to be seen at their best the room must be darkened completely. It is not unusual for training rooms to have curtaining which is insufficient to provide the blackout necessary or which have gaps or holes allowing sunlight to penetrate and ruin the screen image. Changing the lighting state by darkening the room will also have a number of other repercussions:

1. It will mean that eye contact cannot be made with the group. This absence of eye contact makes it all the more essential that the slides are impressive and the narrative stimulating.
2. To avoid disrupting the course too much the slides will need to be shown together as a block rather than where relevant (as is the case with OHP transparencies).
3. Unlike transparencies it is not possible to point items out on a slide. So it will be necessary to use a pointer for darkened rooms. It is possible to get one with a red bulb tip. A word of warning though – using a pointer causes a transformation in trainers and before long they become conductors waving their batons. Use pointers only where necessary, and when they are no longer needed put them down.
4. Finally, in the dark it becomes all the more essential that you are familiar with the training room and equipment. It is difficult to impress people with your professionalism when you trip over extension cabling, fumble for lost remote controls and attempt to read your notes in semi-darkness.

*Do* use slides correctly.

Slides can last for years if mounted and stored correctly. Take time to number each slide so that it is apparent what order they should be in or if any are missing.

It is worth investing in a spare set of slides because there is a tendency for slides to be used in other presentations or to become lost or damaged. If you are using a large number of slides keep these in indexed boxes and compile a numerical list for easy referencing.

*DON'T*

*Don't* become dependent on slides.

The danger of becoming dependent on visual media is greater with slides than with transparencies because a darkened room effectively prevents using notes anyway. This does not mean that notes can be ignored and preparation is unnecessary. Whenever electrical equipment is used there is a risk of breakdowns or blown fuses. Your training shouldn't come to a halt just because your projector has.

*Don't* use slides just because you have them.

It is always tempting, once slides have been compiled, to find opportunities to incorporate them into a training course whether they are wholly relevant or not. The attitude seems to be 'we've paid for all these slides and equipment, we might as well use them'. The weakness of this approach is that it leads to training courses being designed around the equipment and not the other way about. Visual support should enhance any message not dilute it. Don't use visual support just because it's there.

*Don't* use too many slides.

Unless the slide presentation is to illustrate a process or procedure keep the number of slides to a minimum. This will not only keep the costs down but it will maintain a high level of concentration when they are shown. The rule is keep it simple: a limited number of slides and the essential information the group needs to know.

The approach should be :

One idea – One slide – One per minute

### Advantages and disadvantages of slides

| Advantages | Disadvantages |
|---|---|
| Stimulating media | Requires darkened room |
| Adds professionalism | Not flexible |
| Slides are portable | Not possible to change order |
| Suitable for any | during presentation |
| size of group | Equipment can fail |

*Applications*

Ideal for formal training or presentation of facts and figures. Can illustrate a sequence of events in a logical, easily absorbed manner.

### Models

The use of a physical object as a visual aid is vastly underrated and yet it is one of the simplest and most effective forms of visual support. It can be anything from a scaled-down version of a motor engine to a skeleton used for First Aid training. Whatever form it takes make sure that it demonstrates the point it was created for and don't let it undermine the learning point that you wish to make.

### Advantages and disadvantages of models

| Advantages | Disadvantages |
| --- | --- |
| Economical (in most cases) | Can distract group |
| Easy to use | Time consuming to make |

*Application*
Models help the group to visualize concepts difficult to grasp, such as a chemical molecule. Excellent in situations where the original item would be too big, dangerous or costly to produce.

## Audio

As well as visual support it can sometimes be useful to use audio equipment to enhance training. The best example of this is using recording equipment for telephone technique training.

### Advantages and disadvantages of audio equipment

| Advantages | Disadvantages |
| --- | --- |
| Adds novelty and impact | Can be costly |
| Shows strengths and weaknesses clearly | Might be time consuming |
| Can be stopped and started at relevant points | |

| Applications | |
| --- | --- |
| Public address training | Broadcasting skills |
| Evacuation procedure | Telephone techniques |

## Video

The use of video as a means of providing visual support has increased dramatically over the last few years. There are two ways in which using video can assist the trainer. First, by providing a pre-recorded training film for the course. Second, as a means of showing a contemporaneous record of a trainee's actions on the course.

### Video training films

In its first form the video acts as an alternative to films or slides. As training videos have become more popular the range and quality of videos has risen. Today it is likely that there will be a very real choice of videos using well-known actors, and on any topic from general time management to more specialist health and safety requirements.

As well as the major training video providers there are also a number of trade associations who have produced their own training films.

Many large concerns have also subsidized their own training by making videos and these can often be hired out to other interested parties at a nominal charge.

### Advantages and disadvantages of video training films

| Advantages | Disadvantages |
| --- | --- |
| Entertaining | Not always relevant |
| Informative | Expensive to make or hire |
| Memorable | Requires TV monitor and |
| Suitable for medium size | video equipment |
| groups (10-20) | Often regarded as means of |
| | 'filling in' gaps in course |

*Applications*

Video training packages exist on most topics but care should be taken to preview the material before hire. Many are out of date or irrelevant. It is often cheaper to buy outright than to hire for a number of showings.

### Video feedback

The pace of modern technology has meant that video camera equipment is now within the capability and budget of most training departments. This in turn opens up whole new vistas to the trainer. Where previously a participant had been told by the trainer about any verbal or non-verbal idiosyncrasies now, video feedback offers irrefutable proof of performance.

### Techniques on using video feedback

*DO'S*

*Do* keep feedback relevant.

The rule should be that unless the feedback is of general interest only the individual concerned should watch the video playback. Watching somebody else's performance is never as exciting as watching your own and seeing the whole group again can be very monotonous. One solution is to break the group into smaller units and record and critique a unit at a time. Alternatively, involve everyone in the feedback process by giving out a checklist of the main learning points being watched for and ask each group member for a rating or comment.

*Do* monitor the recording.

Check from time to time that the material is being recorded correctly. It's too late to discover the lens cap was left, on when you come to play the videotape back. It is also worth making a note of the digital read-out at the beginning and end of each performance, along with any points worth mentioning to the group/individual later.

Many cameras have the capacity to record the time on the tape and this will greatly assist in finding the relevant material.

*DON'TS*
*Don't* over-emphasize the camera.
Many people find the concept of being video-recorded very intimidating.

The build-up you give can radically affect the performance that *they* give. The ideal approach is to put their minds at ease by concentrating on the *procedures* being recorded and not the recording itself.

## TRAINER'S TIP

Make sure that prior to recording everything is set up and focused as you would like. There should be no reason to distract everybody during recording by fine tuning, zooming or adjusting. Keep movement to a minimum. Attention should be drawn to what is going on in front of the camera and not behind it.

*Don't* over-use video recording.
The video camera can be a very powerful visual medium but it has to be used selectively if it is to retain its impact. Used correctly it can be an incisive tool; used incorrectly it becomes a blunt instrument.

### Advantages and disadvantages of video feedback

| Advantages | Disadvantages |
|---|---|
| Objective viewpoint | Equipment can malfunction |
| Instant recall | Requires some technical |
| Constructive | knowledge |
| Suitable for all sizes of group | Fear factor – use can cause anxiety |

*Applications*
Excellent for role play (interviewing, counselling), interpersonal skills, simulations, and presentations.

Not limited to a linear approach. Can be used for interactive processes such as discussion groups, problem-solving and business games.

► CHAPTER REVIEW ◄

1. A *good* picture is worth a thousand words.

2. Visual aids make good servants but bad masters.

3. Visual aid should supplement your presentation and not the other way round.

4. Visual media are four times more powerful than words alone and considerably more memorable.

5. *When to use* visual support:
   - When the subject matter is complex
   - Where comparisons are necessary
   - Where statistical data is involved
   - To provide reinforcement
   - To maintain interest

6. *What to use* depends on:
   - Subject matter
   - Group size
   - Cost
   - Facilities

| MEDIUM | ADVANTAGES | DISADVANTAGES | APPLICATIONS |
|---|---|---|---|
| FLIP CHART | Easy to use<br>Economical<br>Instant visuals<br>Versatile<br>Capable of advance preparation<br>Can be created by group | Difficult to write at speed<br>Can be cumbersome to use | Recording group's feedback<br>Providing a summary<br>Highlighting key points<br>Suitable for groups of 30 or less |
| WHITEBOARDS | Easy to use<br>Easy to correct<br>Uses colour<br>Economic | Requires special markers<br>Associated with school<br>Non-portable<br>Reflective surface can be difficult to read<br>No permanent record once erased | As with Flip charts<br>Suitable for groups of approximately 30 |
| OVERHEAD PROJECTORS (OHP) | Used in normal lighting conditions<br>Fairly simple to operate<br>Can be transported<br>Transparencies can be prepared in advance and carried easily<br>Economical | Can be distracting or noisy<br>Prone to bulb/machine failure<br>Needs screen/white wall<br>Minimum projection – distance 3-4 metres | Pictorial or diagrammatic data<br>*Small* amounts of text<br>Suitable for most size of group |
| 35mm SLIDES | Stimulating<br>Adds professionalism<br>Slides are portable | Requires blacked out or darkened room<br>Not flexible<br>Cannot change slide order during presentation<br>Equipment can fail | Ideal for formal training<br>Facts and figures<br>Suitable for any size of group |
| MODELS | Economical (generally)<br>Easy to use | Can be distracting<br>Time consuming to make | Where concepts difficult to grasp<br>Where original object too big, dangerous or costly to make available |
| VIDEO TRAINING FILMS | Entertaining<br>Informative<br>Memorable | Not always relevant<br>Expensive to make or hire<br>Requires TV monitor<br>Can be seen as 'filling in' time | Best for groups 10 - 20 in size |
| AUDIO | Adds novelty and impact<br>Shows strengths and weaknesses<br>Can be paused | Can be costly<br>Can be time consuming | Public address training<br>Evacuation procedures<br>Broadcasting skills<br>Telephone techniques |

**Table 12.1** *Review of audio-visual aids*

# *13* Evaluating Training

▷               **SUMMARY**               ◁

This chapter:
- Contrasts evaluation and measurement.
- Explains the importance of evaluation.
- Establishes what evaluation is and how to implement it successfully.

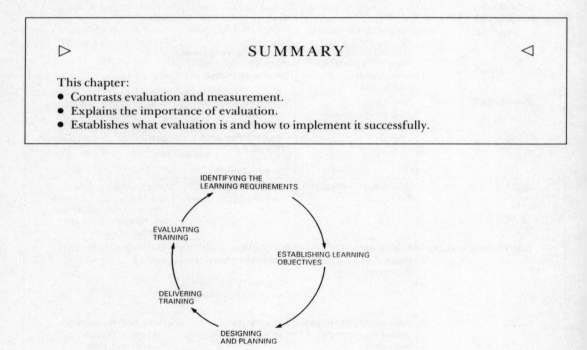

**Figure 13.1** *The training cycle – evaluation*

The evaluation of training forms the remaining part of the training cycle which starts with the identification of the problem, proceeds through the diagnostic phase, where it is classified as a training issue, and continues through to the design and delivery of the training course itself (see Fig. 1.1 on page 16).

It is the function of evaluation to assess whether the learning objectives originally identified have been satisfied and any deficiency rectified. Evaluation then is where a judgement is made about the effectiveness of the training provided.

## The Difference between Evaluation and Measurement

Evaluation and measurement are often regarded as synonymous but although the two are linked, they are not the same thing. *Measurement* is the process of ascribing a numerical value to different aspects of a training event. It is concerned with getting data about the course. *Evaluation*, on the other hand, is where some form of judgement is made about the course.

In most cases, this judgement will be based on the data obtained during the measurement process but this isn't essential. It is possible to come to a conclusion or make a judgement about an issue without ever knowing the facts. There are even occasions where the data can confuse rather than clarify. So, for example, it is still valid to make a decision about whether a meal is enjoyable or not without going to the lengths of measuring the size of the steak or counting the number of potatoes on the plate. However, where such judgements are made, it should be recognized that these will be based on personal preferences and therefore can vary from person to person.

## Why Evaluate?

There are four parties who share a common interest in evaluating the results of any training. These are: the trainer, the trainee, the training and development department, and the client/manager.

### The Trainee

The trainee's interest in any evaluation is a self-centred one. He or she will want to confirm that the course has met his or her personal expectations and aspirations as well as satisfying any learning objectives established by the training department at the beginning of the programme.

### The Trainer

Although the trainer's concern isn't completely altruistic, his or her prime concern is to ensure that the training that has been provided is

167

the most effective training possible under the circumstances. If the results fall short of the standard set, the trainer will need to know in order to modify his or her approach or amend the material.

## The Training and Development Department

The department responsible for the provision of the training will need to determine whether the course has made the best use of the resources available. These resources include people, finance, time, and facilities.

## The Client/Manager

The line manager for the trainee will be seeking reassurance that the time that the trainee has spent attending training was of significant value and that where there was a deficiency in skills or knowledge this has now been redressed.

It can therefore be seen that as well as sharing a common interest in the *need* for evaluation there is also a broad overlap in the information sought by these four parties.

### Objectives satisfied

Close attention will be paid to whether the deficiency in performance (originally diagnosed as a problem rectifiable by training) has now been corrected.

### Full use of resources

Everyone will want confirmation that time and money has not been squandered on unproductive training. The best means of assuming that this isn't the case is to determine the cost/value ratio of the training programme. This should take account of the time spent 'off the job' as well as the cost of providing the training and any miscellaneous expenditure such as accommodation and other expenses.)

### Optimum training

It is equally important that complete advantage is taken of the training opportunity and that the maximum learning is obtained. This will mean examining the course in detail and identifying any strengths or weaknesses highlighted.

### Personal benefit

Irrespective of the contribution made to the training, all the parties will want to feel some element of personal benefit. The trainee will need to believe that he or she has gained by the training experience. The trainer will be seeking confirmation that his or her skills were responsible for any learning achieved. The client/manager will be hoping that the development of skills or knowledge will result in an improvement in the quality or quantity of the work within his area. While those involved in the training and development function will receive some reflected glory and evidence that their efforts are justified.

It might be argued that this ability to provide hard data to substantiate the accomplishment achieved through training would be reason enough to evaluate training, and yet evaluation is still the exception rather than the rule.

## Why People Don't Evaluate

If evaluation is so important why is it that evaluation is carried out so rarely and with such reluctance? Some of the reasons given for *not* evaluating are:

### Cost

Undertaking an evaluation of a training programme can be a costly and time-consuming affair. This doesn't mean that high costs are inevitable and it certainly isn't a valid reason for not evaluating at all. Undoubtedly the costs of providing *ineffectual* training are considerably greater than the costs of *assessing* the results of that training. It is always more expensive to get things wrong than it is to take time to get things right.

### Difficulty

One reason frequently voiced for not carrying out an evaluation is the difficulty in finding a suitable basis for judgement. It is difficult to assess improvements in morale, greater motivation, increased team spirit or heightened self-esteem. All of this, of course, is true but that doesn't make it impossible to evaluate, just very awkward.

If it isn't possible to define the behaviours or activities which the training is seeking to achieve and to identify when the aims have been met then there really doesn't seem to be a great deal of logic in running the training.

### Lack of Interest

It has to be said that it is considerably more enjoyable designing and developing new training programmes than spending time and effort evaluating the success or otherwise of past training courses. This might

**169**

be an understandable point of view but it isn't a legitimate reason for non-evaluation.

### Lack of Credibility

This arises where people find it difficult to place any reliance on the evaluation. This has more to do with the instrument or method selected than it does with the process of evaluation itself.

### Lack of Commitment

As a general rule the lack of effective evaluation can frequently be attributed to a form of corporate inertia. In all other areas, management will not just request but demand hard statistical evidence that the department produces results. Sales departments for example will be expected to demonstrate their contribution to the 'bottom line', while marketing sections will be exhorted to 'yield a good return on investment'. Only in the field of training does it seem possible to substantiate achievement by doing nothing more than confirming the number of courses run and the number of delegates in attendance.

As more and more companies become conscious of the need to provide effective training it is likely that this trend will change and that those responsible for training and development will be required to justify what they do in the face of finite resources.

## Evaluation Process

The evaluation of a training programme is not an exact science and there are as many approaches to assessing success as there are routes to achieving it. In most cases the method of evaluation selected will depend on the nature of the course involved.

This can be simplified by classifying the courses into three different categories depending on their principal purpose. These are:

1. Skills acquisition.
2. Changing attitudes and behaviour.
3. Acquisition of knowledge.

In each category evaluation will form the final step, although the stages which must be passed through to arrive at this position will vary considerably.

| Skills Acquisition | Changing Attitudes and Behaviour | Acquision of Knowledge |
|---|---|---|
| 1. Establish the extent of any skills deficiency | 1. Isolate the attitudes and behaviours soughts | 1. Identify areas where a gap in knowledge exists |
| 2. Assess current standards of performance | 2. Incorporate these into learning objectives | 2. Assess the level of knowledge already possessed |
| 3. Set desired standards of performance | 3. Provide a means of measuring achievement against these learning objectives | 3. Determine level of knowledge required (learning objectives) |
| 4. Undertake training | 4. Conduct change programme | 4. Provide training intervention |
| 5. Measure any change in performance | 5. Assess trainees using chosen measure | 5. Measure any increase or decrease in ability |
| 6. **Evaluate – to establish whether the perceived deficiency has been reduced or eliminated** | 6. **Evaluate – to establish if trainees acquired and continue to demonstrate the prescribed attitudes and behaviours** | 6. **Evaluate – to establish whether the knowledge as been acquired and retained** |

**Table 13.1** *Stages towards evaluation*

## Guidelines for Evaluation

If training is to be judged with any degree of accuracy it is important that the evaluation is based on information which fulfils certain preconditions.

### Relevant Criteria

The criteria selected for evaluation must provide an insight to the effectiveness of the training. This means that details of how many courses have been run, how many delegates attended, or what the topics covered were, may be useful but they won't help assess whether any learning took place.

### Reliable

Clearly there is little point in evaluating information which cannot be relied on but often this lack of reliability is the consequence of bad planning rather than a deliberate attempt to mislead. For example, inconsistencies in the way that an evaluative instrument is applied can dramatically effect the results obtained. This means that any questionnaire, test or assessment should seek the same information from each training group and ask for it in the same manner and in an identical format.

If a system of scoring is required this should be as specific as possible avoiding imprecise or ambiguous terms.

Care should be taken to eliminate any confusion on the part of the participants and any subjectivity on the part of the marker.

## Validity

'Valid' in this context means that where the evaluation is based on some form of measurement, this measure must establish a relationship of cause and effect. In simple terms this means that, even though there might be some measurable change in behaviour following a training programme this change could be the consequence of a number of different factors and not necessarily the consequence of training. If, for example, there had been a recent accident in the workplace arising from the failure to follow the correct safety procedure, this might have a greater impact upon trainees and heighten their awareness independently of any safety training. Any measurement purporting to show the effectiveness of training might be distorted by this factor. It will be apparent from the above example that isolating the effects directly attributable to training from the myriad of other possible causes can be a difficult and complex affair.

## Practical

Merely because evaluation is based on hard data doesn't mean that that instrument of measurement should be hard to understand and apply.

The time and effort required to administer any method must be in proportion to the value of the data that it provides. It is unlikely that a small 'one off' training course will warrant the cost of extensive interviews or justify the time spent completing a twenty-six page questionnaire. If on the other hand the training programme being undertaken forms part of a corporate-wide multi-national change programme, this is far more likely to justify the costs of focus groups and feedback questionnaires.

# What to Evaluate

The purpose of any training evaluation is to examine the training provided and determine how effective that training has been. The problem is that while everyone agrees that this is a perfectly straightforward and laudable objective, it makes little sense until we define what we mean by 'effective'. Is effectiveness providing a training programme that participants enjoy or is it one in which they feel that they have achieved a greater understanding?

Donald Kirkpatrick, in *Training and Development Handbook*, found that a convenient method of analysing evaluation was to divide it into four different categories: reaction; learning; behaviour; and results.

Of these four categories, the most common form of evaluation is one based on the trainees reactions to the programme. This might be the simplest to carry out but the assessment is at best only a broad indication of effectiveness. In order to obtain the complete impact of any training programme all four categories should be evaluated.

## TRAINER'S TIP

Where the course evaluation is going to be based on a form or questionnaire completed by the trainees, then the questions asked must be selected carefully. It can often be easier to look at the evaluative process in reverse and to start by identifying what the purpose of the evaluation is (i.e. to demonstrate behaviourial change, show achievement of specified learning objectives, etc.).

Once this has been established it is then possible to develop questions which will elicit the information you require. Remember the answers you get will depend on the questions you ask. Make certain that any questions you ask are 'open' and allow the respondent to answer freely. Where any question calls for comments or opinion from the trainee, ensure that adequate room is left for the answer and that an indication is given that signing the questionnaire is optional. The anonymity that this provides will ensure that the answers given are an honest reflection of those attending.

## Reaction Evaluation

*Description*
Reaction evaluation provides an analysis of trainee's attitudes towards a specified training programme.

*Application*
This means that reaction evaluation can be a useful means of gauging how trainees feel, particularly about hygiene and maintenance factors such as the quality of training or the standard of the venue which calls for personal impressions.

Areas where reaction evaluation can be especially perceptive includes

| | |
|---|---|
| reaction to course content | use of visual support |
| effect of the trainer's delivery | suitability of facilities |
| appropriateness of learning objectives | degree of participation |
| | level of understanding |
| clarity of handouts | relevance to work |

### Reaction evaluation strengths and weaknessess

*Strengths*

It is important to have a measure which provides some insight into the disposition of trainees (statistical data alone cannot provide the complete picture).

Enjoyment provides increased motivation to learn. If the trainer can ensure that the course is enjoyable then any learning points will become more memorable.

*Weaknesses*

Merely because a training course is enjoyable doesn't mean that anything has been learnt.

Reactions are not an indication that anything has been learnt or that behaviour will change subsequently.

Feelings may be distorted. Trainees might respond with the impression they feel they *ought* to convey rather than with their own views.

It is difficult to make comparisons based on an emotional response. The difference between 'exceptional' and 'adequate' can be marginal in reality and depend solely upon an individual's preconceptions.

## TRAINER'S TIP

1. The views, opinions and feelings of those participating in training programmes can play a significant role in shaping future courses and in deciding on the receptivity of existing training and development. This is particularly true in situations where senior management of an organization are likely to reach conclusions about the adequacy of training based on the comments of those attending the course.

2. When analysing reactive data it is important to keep things in perspective. It is very easy to forget that all comments are perceptual and that minor criticisms should be seen in proportion to the general response.

## Learning Evaluation

### Description

Learning evaluation is a means of confirming that certain facts, skills or principles were communicated to trainees and that a minimum standard of proficiency was achieved.

### Application

In order to establish that learning has taken place it is necessary to assess the quality and quantity of learning derived from the training course.

The best method of evaluating progress of course participants is by reviewing the original learning objectives of the course and then incorporating these into some form of assessment procedure for the trainees.

So, for example, where the course objectives requires proficiency at certain specified skills, the most convenient means of measuring improvement would be to ask trainees to provide a demonstration of the appropriate skills.

In this way a course on interviewing skills might require the trainees to participate in a role play, while an effective speaking course might call on trainees to make a presentation to the group. The same process can be used to monitor the acquisition of skills ranging from boiler maintenance to reading skills.

When organized and implemented, systematically performance-testing before, during and after training can provide the trainer with an accurate and objective measure of the learning process. Unfortunately, while an assessment based on the trainees' ability to perform certain tasks might be appropriate, for skill-based training it isn't appropriate where the objective of the course is to acquire knowledge. Where principles and procedures are the purpose of the training then it is necessary to introduce a more formalized system for testing understanding. In most cases this will be a written test, generally a straightforward 'paper and pencil' test, although multiple choice or comprehension tests are also popular. In other situations an oral assessment may seem more relevant. Whatever the form used, testing trainees is a complex subject and one which requires careful planning, structuring and statistical measurement. Consequently, wherever possible professional help or advice should be sought before implementing any testing procedure.

### Learning evaluation strenghts and weaknesses

*Strengths*
Learning evaluation provides an effective means of monitoring a trainee's progress.

*Weaknesses*
People learn by their mistakes and testing can discourage trainees from trying out new methods or approaches because of the stigma attached to failing.

Where tests are used there is strong pressure from management to make the results 'public' or to use them as the basis of pay and promotion. In either case this pressure must be resisted. Successful training can only take place in a risk-free environment.

Evaluation of learning is no indication that this knowledge will be transferred to the working environment.

## Behavioural Evaluation

*Description*
The purpose of behavioural evaluation is to verify that what has been learnt in training has not only been absorbed by the trainee but is reflected in a change in his or her behaviour.

*Application*
The information obtained from an evaluation of behaviour can be indispensable. It is only by undertaking such an analysis that it is possible to state with any certainty that what has been learnt in training has led to a change in working practices. (It is not unknown for attendees on a course to know all the right answers in the training room but to be totally incapable of putting them into effect in the business environment.)

The only means of confirming that the correct approach extends to the working environment is by monitoring behaviour in the work place. Unfortunately, this is not an easy task to accomplish. One reason for this is that it is difficult to measure 'normal practice' when the very act of observation makes people behave differently. If the results are to have any validity, any assessment should take place when the trainee is not conscious of being monitored.

It is also impossible to verify any change without first taking a pre-course measurement to act as a comparison. In practice, this can often be achieved by a 'before and after' questionnaire which requires the trainee's line manager, direct reports or peers to answer a series of questions on behaviour-related issues.

### Behavioural evaluation strengths and weaknesses

*Strengths*

Ensures that the training is capable of being transferred to the work place and discourages training for training's sake.

Provides for an assessment of the trainee's performance by managers or non-trainers.

*Weaknesses*

Difficult to develop appropriate methods for recording and measuring behaviourial change.

Evaluation needs to be unobtrusive or the process of observation will distort the results.

## Results Evaluation

*Description*

Evaluation by results is an assessment based upon the one factor that every manager recognizes – cost effectiveness.

*Application*

For companies to continue investing in training they must be convinced that the financial commitment that they make to training will produce a very real benefit to the organization. The attitude is that while the pursuit of knowledge in its own right might well be very commendable, the company is more concerned with any financial advantages that will follow as a consequence of any training undertaken. This means that providers of training must demonstrate that there is a clear relationship between the course objectives and the company's profitability.

Improved skills should increase performance, reduce wastage and lower costs. Similarly, induction training should reduce assimilation time, increase job satisfaction, lower staff turnover and add to profits. Whatever the nature of the course it should be possible to justify its purpose in terms of cost/benefits. The company view is often that the company exists to show a profit and only training that contributes towards the financial objectives should be encouraged.

### Results evaluation strengths and weaknesses

*Strengths*

Expresses training in terms which senior management can understand

and relate to.

Hard financial data has greater influence on strategy than the appreciation of those trainees who attended the course.

*Weaknesses*

Accurately assessing the cost benefits of training is not always easy. This is particularly so where softer issues are involved. For example, evaluating how much of a company's increased profits can be ascribed to improved communication can require a complicated analysis.

Not all enterprises are motivated exclusively by profit. Medical facilities exist primarily to restore health or save lives and evaluating medical training on a purely financial basis would be unfair.

# When to Evaluate

Selecting the right time to evaluate training can have a significant effect on the results obtained. In general evaluation will be undertaken at any one of the following stages: pre-course; post-course; or post-post-course. Whichever means is selected it doesn't preclude the use of evaluations at other times (and it could even be argued that a good trainer will be evaluating the course while it is under way).

## Pre-course Evaluation

Evaluations based on measurements taken before the course commences can be a useful means of ascertaining the trainee's level of knowledge prior to the course. In this way it is possible to design the course to take account of this knowledge and to ascertain that when the learning objectives *are* developed they realistically reflect what is achievable.

This level will also form a convenient starting point or base line for monitoring the trainee's progress towards satisfying these learning objectives. In fact, to ensure that the method of evaluation is consistent with the course's learning objectives, the appropriate techniques for evaluation should be considered immediately after setting objectives at the programme design stage.

## Post-course Evaluation

In the majority of cases where an evaluation takes place, it does so at the very end of the training course. This is not in itself a bad thing because trainees are in a much better position to assess how much they have learnt by reviewing the whole training experience. However, in practice, seeking an evaluative response in the last few minutes of a training course can lead to distorted feedback, as trainees, anxious to get home, respond hastily with ill-considered comments or with a view based on a limited recall.

A more effective method of evaluation in the end session is to incorporate a review of the material covered on the course together with a final opportunity to test understanding and gauge progress with a last role play, presentation, demonstration or practice. Once this has been carried out an evaluation indicating what the trainees feels they have learnt and the applicability of this new information to their work can be a worthwhile exercise (see e.g. Figure 13.2).

## Post-post-course Evaluation

The provision of training is an area where the benefits to the company and to the individual can only really be appreciated over a period of time. To gain a more accurate picture of a training programme's success it can often be useful to send out a second questionnaire 4 - 6 weeks after completion of a course, seeking an assessment of the training's value.

The recipient of the questionnaire can either be the trainee or the trainee's line manager, depending on the information sought. The line manager will be able to assess the perseverance of behaviours encouraged during the training, while the trainee will be in a better position to consider how the training relates to the realities of the working environment.

A well-structured post post-course evaluation can provide a valuable indicator of :

— The feasibility of the original learning objectives.
— The practical impact of skills and knowledge communicated.
— The degree of support and reinforcement provided by others.
— Whether the line manager or others could also benefit from attending the training.

**Reaction Sheet** (using different rating methods)
Date ................................................................ Venue ..............................................
Course title ....................................... Trainer ...........................................
Please help us to evaluate our training by giving your reactions and comments.

Content:
1. Did the content meet your personal training requirements?
   To a large extent .........
   To some extent .........
   Very little .........

2. How would you rate the following? 4 (very good) – 1 (very poor)

| | 1 | 2 | 3 | 4 |
|---|---|---|---|---|
| Relevance | | | | |
| Informative | | | | |
| Practical | | | | |

3. How would you assess the trainer's presentation?
   1   2   3   4   5
   ................................................
   Poor                    Excellent

4. How would you grade the following? (Circle appropriate response)
   Use of visual support   1  2  3  4  5
   Course material         1  2  3  4  5
   Training facilities     1  2  3  4  5
                           Poor      Good

5. To what extent did the chapter meet its objectives? (Shade the triangle)

   very little                    completely

6. What parts were the most useful? (Give reasons)
7. Which parts were the least beneficial? (Explain why)
8. How do you think you will use these skills on returning to work?
   1. ............................................
   2. ............................................
   3. ............................................

9. What is your overall assessment?
   ☺ enjoyable
   😐 O.K.                    😐
   ☹ Waste of time

10. Any other comments. ...............................................
........................................................................
Name: (optional) ...................................................

**Figure 13.2** *A sample reaction sheet*

# CHAPTER REVIEW

▶ ◀

*Measurement* is a means of gathering data and ascribing a numerical value to different aspects of training.

*Evaluation* is the process of reaching a judgement about the training based on the measurement data or other criteria.

Evaluation is important to the:

1. Trainee.

2. Trainer.

3. Training and development department.

4. Client/manager.

They will want to ensure that:

1. Objectives are satisfied.

2. Full use is made of resources.

3. Optimum training is provided.

4. Some personal benefit is obtained.

Evaluation can be rejected because it is:

costly              uninteresting         unsupported
difficult           unreliable

If undertaken the evaluation must be:

relevant                     valid
reliable                     practical

There are four stages of evaluation:

1. reactions

2. learning

3. behaviour

4. results

All four should be undertaken to provide a comprehensive view of training.

There are three possible opportunities to undertake an evaluation:

Pre-course      Post-course      Post-post-course

# *14* Checklists

> ▷         SUMMARY         ◁
>
> - Checklists, although not exhaustive, should provide a useful foundation for most training courses, both internal and external.
> - The checklists include:
>   1. Venue and Accommodation Requirements.
>   2. Joining Instructions.
>   3. Materials Checklist.
>   4. Audio Visual Support Checklist.
>   5. Pre-course Checklist.
>   6. Course Checklist.
>   7. Post-course Checklist.

## Checklist 1: Venue and Accommodation Requirements (prior to booking)

It is always advisable to check training venues out fully before confirming a booking. Wherever possible this should be done in person by visiting the location and seeking out the answers to the questions posed below.

**Training Rooms** (generally)

- How many rooms are available?    ☐
- Are syndicate/break-out rooms required? Yes/No    ☐
- If yes, how many? . . . . . . . ..    ☐

- Is a room layout obtainable? □
- Are any facilities shared? □
- Which one(s) are suitable for this course? □
- What distractions might exist? □

## Training Room (specific)

Does the room selected have:
- Good soundproofing? □
- Sufficient electrical or natural light? □
- Dimmable lighting? □
- Directionable spotlighting? □
- Curtains/blinds suitable for blackout? □
- Adequate independent ventilation/air-conditioning? □
- Adequate independent temperature control? □
- Comfortable seating? □
- Sufficient electric power points (if so are these accessible; will an extension cable be necessary)? □
- Enough room for you, your equipment and the group? □

## Training room (facilities)

What facilities are provided:
- Flip chart(s) □
- Easels □
- Whiteboards □
- Overhead projector □
- Video player □
- TV/Monitor □
- Video camera □
- Cassette player □
- Extension cables □
- Carousel projector □
- Screens □
- Special requirements ...... □

## Other amenities

- Where are the toilets located? □
- Are there enough for both sexes? □
- Are they accessible to disabled trainees? □
- Is there a lift? □
- Is there access to: – faxes? □
- – telephones? □

– photocopiers? □
– word processors? □
– computers? □

– How are messages communicated? □

## Security

– Is the room secured overnight? □
– Are valuables/personal belongings safe during breaks? □
– Are security passes or entry requirements necessary? □
– If a car park exists are passes needed? □
– Is access to the training room possible outside
  normal working hours? □

## Food and Drink:

– Are both tea and coffee available during breaks? □
– Can break times be varied? □
– Can lunch arrangements be varied? □
– What are lunch arrangements? □
– What is included and what is excluded in the price? □
– Are vegetarian or special dietary meals possible? □
– Is there a bar and if so what are the serving times? □
– Who is responsible for liaising with the course trainer? □

## Location

– Is the venue easily accessible by public transport? □
– Is the venue easily accessible by road? □
– Does a car park exist with enough spaces/ reservations
  for participants? □
– Where rail transport is used can a courtesy bus/car collect
  from the station? □

## If residential

– How many bedrooms are available? □
– Are the rooms single/double? □
– With private facilities? □
– Are soap/towels provided? □
– Is there a table and lamp for course work? □
– Is there a TV and/or radio? □
– Is there a private telephone? □
– Are newspapers available? □

- Are wake-up calls possible? ☐
- Are there tea and coffee making facilities? ☐
- When should delegates check out? ☐
- Is there somewhere to leave luggage
    prior to departure? ☐
- What are the arrangements regarding payment? ☐

**Note:** If the answers to the questions above are satisfactory, confirm the course in writing setting out: date, course details, numbers, catering and equipment requirements, any special needs, desired training-room layout. Clarify costings, enclose any deposit necessary, and agree to finalize details nearer the time (and note in your diary to do so).

# Checklist 2: Joining Instructions (2 weeks before the course)

All prospective participants should receive confirmation of their place on the course and any joining information two weeks before the course starts. These instructions should include:

- Title of course ☐
- Date(s) course taking place ☐
- Check-in or registration time ☐
- Starting time (if different) ☐
- Where to report on arrival ☐
- Contact name and telephone number
    (in case of difficulties) ☐
- Address and location ☐
- Road map/travel details, including nearest station/bus/
    courtesy bus times or timetables and (where appropriate)
    car park facilities ☐
- Whether residential/non-residential ☐
- If residential incorporate:
    - room details (if available) ☐
    - hotel brochure ☐
    - hotel telephone number ☐
    - explanation of facilities (bar, pool, gym, sauna,
        public telephone) ☐
- checking out times ☐
- payment arrangements ☐
- nearest shops/bank/post-office ☐
- what is included and what is excluded in the costs ☐
- Contact name and telephone numbers at venue
    for messages – state if public telephone available for
    external calls. ☐

      – Meal arrangements and whom to notify
         if dietary alterations required.      ☐

      – Arrangements and rates for re-imbursing travel
         and subsistence      ☐

      – Course outline or programme      ☐

      – Any pre-course preparation or reading
         (case studies, handouts) necessary      ☐

      – Any course materials not provided. Pads, paper, pens,
         examples of trainee's own work      ☐

      – Any other items needed. Soap, towels, hairdrier,
         outdoor clothing      ☐

      – Whom to contact for further details or
         assistance about the course      ☐

      – Any special instructions      ☐

## Checklist 3: Materials (before the course)

Not all these items will be necessary for every course but it is worth
maintaining a materials box with your own checklist. This should also
contain instructions which emphasize that anything used should be
replaced and if anything is missing/broken the details should be given
to a named person on a telephone number provided.

### Pens

      – Marker pens for flip charts (spirit type). Assorted colours  ☐
      – Marker pens for whiteboard (dry writer). Assorted colours  ☐
      – Pack of OHP pens (non-permanent). Assorted colours  ☐
      – Highlighters  ☐
      – Spare Biros  ☐
      – Spare pencils with erasers  ☐

### General

      – Paperclips  ☐
      – Bulldog clips (min 2 for flip chart. See chapter on
         Visual Support)  ☐
      – Elastic bands  ☐
      – Drawing pins/Blu Tac/ double sided tape  ☐
      – Sellotape  ☐
      – Scissors  ☐
      – Penknife/screwdriver/Stanley knife  ☐

- Ruler ☐
- Calculator ☐
- Stopwatch/clock ☐
- Two or fourhole paper punch ☐
- Stapler and staples ☐
- File covers/envelope files ☐
- Name badges ☐
- Tent cards (for participants' names) ☐
- 'No Smoking' signs ☐
- Spare transparencies/acetate roll (see Visual Support list) ☐

## Paper

- Note pads ☐
- Spare paper ☐
- Scrap pads ☐
- Spare flip chart pads ☐

# Checklist 4: Audio Visual Support (before the course)

## Overhead Projectors

- Spare bulb ☐
- Acetate roll ☐
- Transparencies ☐
- Transparency table, check suitable surface exists to lay out transparencies ☐
- Pointer ☐
- Screen ☐
- Platen and lens cleaner – use white spirit or non-smear glass cleaner ☐
- OHP trolley to hold OHP ☐
- OHP Pens (assorted colours) ☐

## Video

- Video player:
  - check compatible format ☐
  - check suitable remote control ☐
  - check batteries in remote control ☐
- Video cassettes:
  - If pre-recorded, check rewound if used previously ☐

**187**

- If blank, check tape time available is
  sufficient for purpose intended (30, 60, 90, 180 mins) ☐
- Video camera: ☐
  - ensure instructions available ☐
  - check white balance if necessary ☐
- TV/Monitor:
  - accurately tuned in ☐
  - screen size appropriate ☐

## Whiteboard

- dry markers (assorted colours) ☐
- pointer ☐
- duster ☐
- cleaning fluid ☐

## Flip Chart

- Flip charts ☐
- If blank, check sufficient number,
  ensure non-bleed paper ☐
- If previously prepared, check correct
  chart, no spelling errors/omissions ☐
- Easel ☐
- Spirit markers (assorted colours) ☐

## Audio

- Cassette player, ensure digital
  counter set to zero ☐
- condenser microphone/suitable microphone available ☐
- blank cassette, check duration
  (60, 90 mins) ☐
- check quality ☐

## Carousel

- Carousel – check slides inserted correctly
  (right order, right way round) ☐
- check infra-red or long lead remote ☐
- spare mounts available ☐
- check projector correctly focused ☐
- check lens clean ☐

– Screen – check size and positioning ☐

**Handouts**

– handouts collated correctly and
in sufficient numbers ☐

**Models**

– assembled correctly ☐
– moving parts tested ☐
– adequate power source if required ☐

**Audio Visual Emergency Kit**

Whenever audio visual support material is likely to be used it is worthwhile assembling an emergency kit to cover most eventualities. This should include:

| | |
|---|---|
| Splicing tape | OHP Bulb |
| Sellotape | Extension lead |
| Craft knife | Screwdrivers |
| Scissors | Fuses |
| Spare pens OHP/ spirit/ dry | Penknife |
| Bull dog clips | Spare video/audio cassette |

# Checklist 5: Pre-course (1 week before the course)

**General**

– Confirm final number of participants ☐
– Prepare list of participants ☐
– Prepare badges ☐
– Check accommodation (if appropriate) ☐
– Check travel arrangements ☐
– Check course materials box (see separate checklist) ☐
– Check First Aid equipment (see 'First Aid' in Chapter 5) ☐
– Check and preview any training videos ☐
– Assemble and check slides ☐
– Prepare OHP transparencies ☐
– Check handouts, printed manuals available ☐
– Check any assembled special equipment ☐

**Venue**

– Confirm final numbers attending ☐
– Check arrangements for: ☐

- parking ☐
- reception ☐
- coffee/tea breaks ☐
- lunch ☐
- special dietary requirements ☐
- timings ☐
- Confirm any equipment provided by venue will be available ☐
- Verify room layout ☐

## Guest Speakers

- Brief any internal/visiting speaker about:
  - programme ☐
  - timetable ☐
  - travel arrangements ☐
  - directions ☐
  - requirements ☐
  - visual support equipment available ☐
  - meals and accommodation arrangements ☐

# Checklist 6: Course (on the day – before the course starts)

## Arrival

- Set up reception table ☐
- Set out badges ☐
- Provide list of participants list ☐
- Confirm room location with reception ☐
- Set up direction signs to room ☐
- Check parking places ☐
- Set out table display of books/other courses
  (where appropriate) ☐
- Check tea/coffee/biscuits available
  for participants on arrival ☐
- Confirm timings for coffee/lunch/tea breaks ☐
- Confirm numbers for coffee/lunch/tea ☐
- Check no fire drills expected ☐

## Room

- Check room layout ☐
- Check sufficient seating (including spare chairs

for observers/late arrivals) ☐
- Check whereabouts of controls for:
    - heating ☐
    - ventilation ☐
    - lighting ☐
- Set out folders ☐
- Set out pens ☐
- Set out tent cards ☐
- Provide marking pens to write names ☐
- Provide 'No smoking' signs/ashtrays ☐
- Check system for relaying messages/message board ☐
- Check location of fire exits/fire extinguishers ☐
- Check clock correct ☐

## Equipment check

Check
- TV monitor ☐
- carousel projector *and* remote ☐
- video player *and* remote ☐
- video camera *and* blank video cassette ☐
- cassette player *and* blank audio cassette ☐
- marker pens ☐
- clean flip chart and easel ☐
- spare flipcharts ☐
- whiteboard and duster ☐
- OHP pens ☐
- OHP projector ☐
- screen ☐
- check blackout curtains/blinds ☐

## Trainer

Check trainer's
- notes ☐
- handouts ☐
- training manuals ☐
- OHP transparencies ☐
- slide carousel ☐
- pens ☐
- pointer ☐
- stopwatch ☐
- clock ☐

## Checklist 7: Post-course

- Review course and arrangements, noting changes for future course ☐
- Amend any file records (Training/Personnel/Course) ☐
- Collate course evaluations ☐
- Prepare report (if necessary) ☐
- Check course material box and replace lost/used/broken items ☐
- Check audio/visual equipment for damage ☐
- Rewind pre-recorded video cassettes ☐
- Return any hired materials ☐
- Arrange for reimbursement of participants' travel and course expenses ☐
- Settle outstanding invoices (deducting any prepayments or deposits) ☐
- Calculate final costs ☐
- Write letters of thanks to venue/speakers ☐
- Follow up any action agreed on the course ☐

## Further Reading

A personal selection to complement and expand on the chapters in this book.

Cristina, Stuart, *Effective Speaking* (1988), Pan.

Custer, G, *Planning, Packaging and Presenting Training* (1984), University Associates.

Goad, Tom, *Delivering Effective Training* (1982), Sabiego, Calif. University Associates.

Kirkpatrick, D L, *Evaluating Training Programs* (1975), American Society for Training and Development.

Laird, Douglas, *Approaches to Training and Development* (1985), Addison Wesley.

Looker, Terry and Gregson, Olga, *Stresswise* (1989), Hodder & Stoughton.

Mager, Robert F, *Preparing Instructional Objectives* (1990), Kogan Page.

Miller, Vincent, *Guidebook for International Trainers in Business and Industry*, (1979), Van Nostrand Reinhold.

Nilson, Carolyn, *Training for Non-Trainers* (1990), AMA.

Pease, Alan, *Body Language* (1984), Sheldon Press.

Pepper, Allan, *Managing the Training and Development Function* (1984), Gower.

Rae, Leslie, *The Skills of Training* (1983), Gower.

Robinson, J and GD, *Training for Impact* (1989), Jossey-Bass.

Robinson, Kenneth, *A Handbook of Training Management* (1981), Kogan Page.

Stuart, Christina, *Effective Speaking* (1988), Pan Books.

Townshend, John, *The Instructor's Pocket Book* (1990), Management Pocket Book Series.

Tuck, Christopher, *Effective Speaking* (1985), E & FN Spon.